Chips, salsa, happiness. We know that essential truth. But after more than 500 years of salsa history, there's so much more to discover about this staple dish, one that cooks today can customize and riff on freely. Salsa can be an irresistible dip, yes, or a flavorful condiment, or it can be the basis for iconic Mexican meals—not to mention a savior for grilled cheese, burgers, rotisserie chicken, or platters of roasted vegetables.

Rick takes us deep into the world of traditional and modern salsas, where a playful pico de gallo with tomatoes, avocados, and chipotles is chopped up in a few minutes, or where you might blend roasted peanuts with caramelized onions and toasted chiles for a nutty-savory spicy sauce. With more than 70 salsa recipes and 24 easy meals that offer endless variation, this book shows you how salsa can catapult joy into your cooking and become the heart of every table.

RICK MARTÍNEZ

SALSA DADDY

Dip Your Way into Mexican Cooking

with Alex Beggs

PHOTOGRAPHS BY ALEX LAU

Clarkson Potter/Publishers
New York

CONT

TENTS

While most of the book is recipes for salsas, Chapter 8 is dedicated to quick and easy meals that either use the salsas from previous chapters, or are ways of making simple food super delicious by being served with any number of salsas. I made salsa recommendations for each dish. I focused on uncomplicated weeknight Mexican dinners, classics like enchiladas and chilaquiles, and some fun surprises near the end . . .

RICK, I'M LOOKING

FOR A SALSA FOR...

INTRO

✳ I'd never had a salsa like this before. It was made up of caramelized onions and chiles serranos, and not much else. But the flavor—where to begin? It hit me like a luchador's full body slam. It combined the sweet depth of the most sublime French onion soup you've ever had—maybe in a dingy bistro on a wobbly table with a red checkered tablecloth—with the smoky and spicy heat of serranos, bringing me solidly back to Mexico. It was lightly blended and pourable, but it was still rich, thick, and warm. I slathered it on my torta and realized: Nothing will be the same after this.

It changed the way I think about salsa. I was in Mexico City at my friend Carlos Ruiz's Taqueria Trompo Imperial. When he served me a football-size torta, he brought out a dozen mismatched clay bowls of salsas to sample. I landed on that caramelized onion salsa and, I'm not kidding, I went home that night and lay in bed, still thinking about it. I could see myself as if from a satellite thousands of miles above Mazatlán, a tiny speck on this planet, where there are infinite possibilities for salsa.

Cooks tend to get set in their ways. If you grew up making your grandmother's pozole rojo with ancho, guajillo, and cascabel chiles, that's how you're going to make it forever. Carrying on tradition is beautiful, if a little intense. And yet when it comes to salsas, I noticed that a lot of Mexicans chill out. They're freer. They experiment and invent. They're in a mindset of uninhibited creativity. After all, the role of any salsa is to complement and catapult the joy of eating. So shouldn't it be a joy to make? When it's time to make salsa, it's time to play. So, let's play.

In my first book, *Mi Cocina*, I explored the diversity of Mexican food across the country. And over and over, readers kept telling me how much they loved the salsa chapter and wished there were even more. I agree! Salsa—not just a dip for chips—is a great gateway into Mexican cooking because it's the base for so many iconic dishes . . . and it goes with so many more.

In *Salsa Daddy,* you'll get to know many different types of salsas, and by extension, different types of chiles, how to tame their heat, how to deepen the flavors of other ingredients, and you'll end up with

a fridge and freezer full of salsas to save you from boring weeknight dinner hell for months and months.

I didn't expect writing this book would fundamentally change me as a cook, but it did. Before, I made salsas to accompany main dishes. It was the second thing, the accessory. But here, I learned to think salsa-first. My imagination went wild. I was pulling ingredients from every corner of the market, flavor combinations popped into my head like hallucinations. I wasn't experimenting as a scientist in a lab, I was playing like a kid. Once the salsa was made, then I'd figure out how to pair it, testing it with all of the daily dishes in my life: breakfast tacos, rotisserie chicken, grilled shrimp, roasted vegetables. Each salsa's versatility felt expansive. What *couldn't* a smoky and creamy chipotle salsa go on? I ate it on everything in sight. And I learned that whether I'm making a traditional Mexican dish, an American one, or even just a basic sandwich or bowl of pasta, that collection of salsas always had a place at the table—and always made things better.

I was cooking with salsa in a new way, too, spooning that caramelized onion salsa into a simple chicken soup (see page 272). I combined the leftovers of two salsas into a pan of fried rice—great. I roasted a chicken smothered in leftover apricot-chipotle salsa (see page 129)—fantastic. I coated a filet of fish in a spicy aioli and broiled it—insane (see page 213). Almost 100 different salsas came and went from my kitchen and I never got bored. When you're feeling overwhelmed by the task of what to make for dinner, it all falls into place if you do one thing: Just make salsa!

What Is a Salsa?

The direct translation of the word *salsa* is "sauce," which is an understatement. In Mexico, salsa is so much more. It's a seasoning for food that tickles and gratifies the palate. An accompaniment that adds depth, poignancy, and zest often in the form of spicy, sweet, and sour flavors. But it's more than a condiment—salsa is a quintessential part of the Mexican table. If you're at your aunt's house, she'll offer you at least two salsas with the tamales she just pulled out of the freezer and microwaved for you. No matter what you are eating, there is a salsa to go with it. I can't eat a taco without it, and neither should you.

While salsa only arrived as a commercial good in the US in the 1980s, salsas have existed long before the arrival of the Europeans in the fifteenth century. The ancient Náhuatl word *molli* was a sauce that was made from grinding or smashing chiles. Mole comes from molli, and is a cooked, ground salsa that, when made well, reaches deep into my soul and latches on. It's earthy and warming, the opposite energy of a bright and punchy pineapple-habanero hot sauce. And yet, they're both salsas.

There's a crisis* in this world of ours, and it's that too many people think in salsa binaries. Red or green? Folks, there are so many more flavors and colors to explore. Have you had salsa blanca? I made one recently with pickled jalapeño, mayo, and herbs, and it was the base of the best damn chicken salad of my life. But I'm digressing. The salsa spectrum is wide and wonderful. That's the range we'll explore here. We'll be charring, blending, and even fermenting. You'll discover salsas to slather on sandwiches, to use as the base of tortilla soup, and to roast chicken in. Rather than making a salsa to go with a main dish, you'll start with a salsa and see where it can take you, far beyond tacos.

Okay this is a minor crisis, but a crisis nonetheless.

There's Salsa de Mesa, and Then There's Everyone Else

Salsa de mesa is your all-purpose table salsa used as a condiment for any- and everything. It's the salsa your parents pass back and forth at the dinner table, or the bowls the restaurant has to keep refilling because you're inhaling endless chips. It's versatile, whereas salsas like mole, pipián, and salsa for enchiladas are used to cook with and have a more specific purpose or pairing. You can definitely break those rules, but it's one way to navigate this book as you distinguish the everyday bowls of salsas (the majority of the book, really) versus the dish-specific ones. Whatever salsa makes you want to have it on-hand at all times is your salsa de mesa.

THE SALSA PANTRY, LEGENDS' ONLY

The truth is, you can make salsa with nearly anything your heart desires. If I teach you one thing in this book, it's to set your expectations free. All the produce in the market is fair game. However, these are the ingredients I reach for again and again in this book, so you might as well get to know each other better.

Tomatoes vs. tomatillos

My bias is that I love a salsa verde and I prefer the acidic, bright rush of a juicy tomatillo over a sweet, ripe tomato (in salsa) most days. If you haven't cooked with tomatillos before, they look like green tomatoes in a papery husk, but they're an entirely different product. Don't worry about picking out the perfect ones or knowing any tricks for ripeness. They'll be firm and a little sticky behind their husk, but don't hold that against them. They're so zingy with acidity that in most of the salsas I use them in, I skip the lime juice (more on that in a bit).

In the tomato department, I always call for Roma tomatoes, the most common in Mexican markets and stores. They're grown here and because of this wonderful sunshine, they're always in season and delicious. I know that's not the case in the US. So when you're shopping for tomatoes for a salsa in this book, work with the best you can get your hands on. If the Romas look pale and sad, look for sweet Campari tomatoes, cherry tomatoes, or those cute on-the-vine ones.

Can I swap for canned tomatoes?

For a salsa that calls for raw or cooked tomatoes, you can use whole canned tomatoes. For salsas with charred tomatoes, you can use fire-roasted, canned tomatoes—they will have the most similar, fire-kissed flavor. If you taste the salsa and it feels a little flat, add a squeeze of lime juice. If you're out of fresh and canned tomatoes, consider another mild and juicy fruit, like plums. Really! I meant it when I said all the produce in the market is fair game.

Can I swap tomatoes for tomatillos?

I realize tomatillos might be harder to find than tomatoes in some places, so yes, you can switch them out with tomatoes, just follow the weight measurements (1 pound of tomatoes/tomatillos, versus the number like 4 or 5). HOWEVER, you can't stop there. I use tomatillos for their acidity, so if you're using tomatoes instead, I'd add a squeeze of lime to the finished salsa to help balance the tomatoes' sweetness. Taste, and add more lime if needed.

Garlic

Obviously. Can't live without it. I use garlic in two different forms in my salsas. In fresh salsas, I use 1 clove of raw garlic to add the sharp bite and heat I need to balance the other ingredients. In salsas *tatemadas* (charred), I use 2 to 3 garlic cloves that I lightly char in a skillet in their skin, which steams and browns it at the same time, and picks up the bitter, charred flavors while developing a lightly roasted garlic sweetness. That said, in your own salsa journey, you can play with mixing and matching the two!

White onions

Not yellow, Vidalia, or red (in most of my recipes). White onions are the gospel of Mexican cooking because they've got a big, clean, crisp bite. It gets in and gets out. Those other onions veer slightly hotter or sweeter and linger. No normal human will notice this difference except for me, but I can't help myself.

Salt

I cook at home with local sea salt. But after years of working in restaurants and test kitchens, I write recipes with Diamond Crystal kosher salt, the industry standard because of its light, airy granules, which make it easier to salt with control and not accidentally oversalt. Morton's kosher salt has much denser grains, so use about half

the volume as what's called for in the recipe if that's in your pantry. One teaspoon of Diamond Crystal is about ½ teaspoon of Morton's. (And then, of course, taste and add more salt if you'd like.) No matter what salt you use, you can follow the ounce or gram weight and you'll be fine, or just salt to taste.

Herbs

Cilantro isn't the only herb for salsa, and tender herbs like basil, parsley, lemon balm, tarragon, and mint are all up for grabs. I like to use just enough herbs for a summer breeze–like freshness, so know that a little can go a long way. Herbs are flavorful, and you want your salsa to be balanced, start with a tablespoon and take it up from there.

Chiles

They deserve their own spread—see Chile Breakdown, pages 16–21.

Chicken bouillon

Every Mexican pantry has a stash of chicken bouillon, usually the yellow jar from Knorr with a red outline of a chicken on it. (Boxed stock isn't really a thing, and good luck finding it at the mercado.) The beauty of that bouillon powder is that there's MSG in it, which oomphs up all the other flavors in the salsa (and at the end of the day, it's a tiny serving of MSG so please relax). In this book, bouillon is used in cooked salsas to bring out their toasty flavor. Raw salsas have enough punch so they don't need it. I don't need MSG in guacamole to eat the whole bowl, ya know?

Fats

Lard (rendered pork fat), is my default cooking oil. It's all about flavor. It has a roasted richness that olive oil can't compete with. I source it locally, and I realize how lucky I am. I describe its flavor as "a kiss of pork." That flavor is a humming baseline in Mexican cuisine. Lard has a bad reputation in the US—let's blame decades of anti-fat dieting—but the truth is, it's lower in cholesterol and saturated fat than butter. I also respect it as part of nose-to-tail butchery, in which every part of the pig is used in some way (lard is typically a by-product of one of my favorite pork products—chicharrones). If you can't access high-quality lard, your leftover bacon or chicken fat is a great substitution, and if you're vegetarian, try a plant-based oil made even more flavorful by frying onion and garlic in it until they are very brown, then straining it to use later. Whatever you do, avoid Crisco and white bricks of hydrogenated lard, which are processed to be extra shelf-stable. We deserve better.

Chipotles in adobo

Chipotles in adobo are dried, medium-size red-ripe jalapeños smoked and cooked in a spiced, tart salsa and canned. They're a genius shortcut to a long-cooked flavor, even if you just use one chile (or its smoky adobo) from the can. Transfer the rest to an airtight container and freeze for later. See them put to good use in the Chipotles en Crema (page 209).

Chicharrones

Fried pork skins. They make me drool like Homer Simpson. They're the perfect vehicle for salsa, and the perfect sponge to soak it up for a satisfying, saucy breakfast (see page 249). I even pulverize some in a salsa called The Crunchy Plum (page 69), which is best eaten with more chicharrones, obvs. I buy my chicharrones from my local mercado, but they're interchangeable with (convenience-store-bought) pork rinds as long as the pork rinds you buy are actually made with pork, not flour and chemicals.

Avocado

Always use soft, ripe avocados, which means surrendering to nature's timeline. Let them sit on the counter until they're ready—your fingers should be able to feel some give when you gently press into the skin—you can't bludgeon an avocado into submission.
Have a slightly underripe avocado and need salsa NOW? Head to: Guacamole con Tomatillos, page 84.

Prickly pear/plums

In Mexico, prickly pear is a familiar salsa ingredient with a bright, lip-puckery tartness mellowed by its plummy, apricot fruitiness. Throughout this book, I'll usually call for plums instead, which have a similar mild sourness. That said, if you have access to prickly pear, go forth and thrive—just match the weights I list for the plum amount.

Sour oranges

Sour oranges are common in Mexico but may be hard to find where you are (though I know some people whose backyard orange trees are pretty sour). Throughout the book you'll see me call for a combination of orange and lime juice (and sometimes zest), which I'm using to mimic the flavor of sour oranges. If you have sour oranges, use them in place of the total amount of juice called for.

Where's the Lime?

I've noticed in my long salsa life that lime juice is almost exclusively used as a salsa ingredient in the US, but not necessarily in Mexico. My theory is it's because American tomatoes tend to be so lackluster they need lime juice to wake them up. And because the Mexican table always has cut limes to accompany every meal. I've also found that the acidity lime brings to salsa can also come from other ingredients, such as tomatillos and vinegar, so I don't use it as often as you'd expect.

CHILE BREAK-DOWN

Fresh chiles

In this book, you'll find hundreds of jalapeños, which I use for their grassy, green flavor and medium heat level. I amp it up with serranos when I want more heat. And I go to habaneros when I'm craving a fruity, tropical heat. Poblanos are for sweet, vegetal heat. When you see the number of chiles called for in a recipe, don't be scared. The heat from the chiles is balanced by the other ingredients in the salsa, and I'll show you how to tame it (see "Capsaicin Corner," page 25). That said, salsa is a study of self-discovery, so if you'd prefer to start with fewer jalapeños and see how it tastes, go for it. This isn't baking, where a change in sugar can throw off a cake's structure, but you may notice other flavors in the salsa come to the forefront.

Dried chiles

If you think of chiles as just a bringer of heat, you're missing the point. They're here for flavor. They're also the reason Mexican cuisine is recognized by UNESCO as a global Intangible Cultural Heritage. Their flavor is intrinsic to Mexican cooking, representing the breadth of our agricultural resources and history, each chile a link to the past, when Mesoamerican societies used chiles for medicinal purposes, religious ceremonies, and to punish bad children. So if you've only messed around with red pepper flakes up until this point, you're in for a treat. (And I promise not to hurt you.)

Dried chiles are often made from fresh chiles that have been fully ripened on their plant (jalapeños turn from green to bright red) to develop their sugars. The process reveals a flavor spectrum as complex as the notes in good coffee, wine, cheese, and whiskey. Heat is a happy by-product. In different chiles, I pick up grassy, fruity,

nutty, herby, chocolatey notes. I used a variety throughout the book to share the love and show this stunning range, but feel free to experiment with whatever you buy to see what stands out to your palate.

Like grapes and raisins, dried chiles have a completely different flavor profile from their fresh counterpart, and have different names (see Meet the Chiles, page 20). A poblano becomes a chile ancho when it's dried, wrinkly, and blackened from the sun. It's mild and sweet, with chocolate and raisin notes, so I often pair it with something hotter for balance. Just don't call the ancho "dried ancho chile"—that's as redundant as saying dried raisin.

Why do you spell chile with an e, not "chili"?

Great question. The word comes from the native Náhuatl word *chilli,* but in Mexico, Spanish-speaking countries, and regions of the US, chile with an e is used to denote the spicy, mild, or sweet peppers, to avoid confusion with American Chili—the meaty stew—made with chili powder.

Buying fresh chiles

Look for jalapeños, serranos, etc., that have firm, shiny flesh with no wrinkles—like someone who just got a lot of work done. The skin should be tight like an apple's.

Buying dried chiles

Look for soft, pliable chiles that indicate they were dried fairly recently. If they're dusty, brittle, and faded, you might as well use chile powder. If your store sells chiles in plastic bags, squeeze through the bag. If the chile crumbles into dust like an untombed mummy, walk away. At home, I refresh my chile stash every January. The dried-out chiles get ground up and turned into mulch. Plants love it, and it'll keep some bugs away.

Toasting dried chiles

Each recipe in this book will guide you on how to prepare your chiles, and most of the time I'm boiling them. This softens them and creates a flavorful, infused liquid. But sometimes in life you want a toasted chile, which deepens its sweetness and smokiness. You could, for example, toast the chiles before boiling them, for an even richer flavor, as in the recipe for Gloria's Chile Colorado (page 264).

In Mexico, chiles are typically toasted on a large comal over an open flame or over high heat on the stove, for 5 to 15 seconds depending on how hot your flame is, and if you are holding them flat on the comal or if they're curled up and only touching the pan in spots. This technique takes practice. If you burn even just a spot on a chile, you'll taste the bitterness, almost like the flavor of charcoal. The good news is, there's a way to toast chiles with less risk of burning them.

Remove the stem and seeds from the chile and toast them in a 350°F oven for 5 minutes. The most important cue is smell and color, not time: When toasted, they'll smell nutty, like toasted paprika, and be slightly darker than they were when you put them in. You'll also see some light brown blistered spots and that is totally normal—exactly what you want. If your oven runs hot, they might be ready in as fast as 3 minutes, so this is not a good time to go and touch up your nails.

You can also toast them in oil, which I do in a couple of places in this book (such as Mole Sencillo, page 178). This creates a different flavor and texture than a dry toast. Think of a piece of toast that you put in a toaster versus one that you toast with butter or olive oil in a cast iron skillet. The latter takes on richness and flavor from the oil, while the other is pure toasted bread.

Bonus: You can even toast chiles over a live fire. I have done this a few times and it was super cool but it was for a mole negro you can find on *New York Times* Cooking—it requires boiling and draining the charred chiles multiple times to wash the ash off. A labor of love, but so worth it!

On chile substituting

When you can't find a chile called for in a recipe, swap with another that's in a similar Scoville range or flavor profile (like anchos for guajillos).

On ground chile substituting

In desperate times, you can use approximately 1 tablespoon of chile powder in place of a whole chile, adding more as necessary. For hotter chiles, use 1 teaspoon red pepper flakes or ½ teaspoon cayenne per whole chile. I wouldn't do this for salsas where the dried chile is the star ingredient (like La Morita, page 102), because the flavors aren't as deep or complex.

A FEW CHILE RULES

1.
The smaller the chile, the hotter it is (generally).

2.
Green chiles will taste grassier, while red will be sweeter and fruitier; both can be spicy.

3.
It's true, sometimes jalapeños are spicier or milder than you expect—the only way to know what you're working with is to taste it.

4.
Always remove the stem and seeds from larger dried chiles (leave the seeds in the little guys for a bigger kick): Wear gloves and use your hands to rip them open like the stem is a gate and shake most of the seeds out.

5.
Wash your hands thoroughly after handling chiles or suffer the consequences (unless you wore gloves).

MEET THE CHILES

POBLANO (*fresh*) → ANCHO OR MULATO (*dried*)

Poblanos are grassy and vegetal and can be spicy as a mild jalapeno. Anchos are larger and meatier, mulatos are smaller and the flesh thinner. Both are a gorgeous deep burgundy/brick red color. The flavor is apricot, cherry, anise, and pimenton. **Heat rating:** 500–3,000 Scoville units, barely a tickle on the tongue.

CHILACA (*fresh*) → PASILLA OR NEGRO (*dried*)

Pasilla are robust with chocolate and coffee flavors with notes of dried hay and caramel. **Heat rating:** 1,000–4,000 Scoville units, barely detectable heat.

MIRASOL GRANDE (*fresh*) → GUAJILLO (*dried*)

Guajillos are fruity, nutty, citrusy, piney, and bright with a little acidity. **Heat rating:** 2,000–5,000 Scoville units, pleasant warmth in smaller quantities.

MIRASOL CHICO (*fresh*) → PUYA (*dried*)

Puya is similar to the guajillo, but fruitier and hotter. **Heat rating:** 5,000–30,000 Scoville units, tingling to intense, depending on luck of the draw.

BOLA (*fresh*) → CASCABEL (*dried*)

Cascabel are earthy and nutty with moderate heat, sometimes like serrano-hot. **Heat rating:** 2,500–8,000 Scoville units, glow with sweat.

JALAPEÑO (*fresh*) → CHIPOTLE (*dried, large*) / MORA (*dried, medium*) / MORITA (*dried, small*)

Jalapeños tend to be milder in the US with grassy, vegetal, herby flavor, and mild heat.

Chipotles are red jalapeños that are fully ripened on the plant; picked; dried in the sun or ovens; then lightly smoked with mesquite, walnut, oak, or pecan (depending on the region). **Heat rating:** 2500–10,000 Scoville units, almost dripping sweat.

CHIPOTLE MECO (*dried*)

This is super-ripe jalapeño, so red it starts to get veiny and slightly leathery looking on the plant. It's picked and dried in the oven or sun and then smoked for up to 48 hours, creating a wide, leathering dried chile with a smoke-pit flavor that's intense. Use sparingly. **Heat rating:** 3,500–10,000 Scoville units, comforting until it's tearful.

GUERO/CARIBE/AMARILLO (*fresh*)

Generally mild but sometimes hot, always thick and fleshy. Notes of clove, allspice, nuts. Great in guisos/soups. Also served charred alongside tacos and Sonoran hot dogs (see page 275). **Heat rating:** 5,000–15,000 Scoville units, mild or madness.

CHILHUACLE AMARILLO (*dried*)

Citrusy and sweet (though not as tropical as a habanero), and as mild as a guajillo. Common in Oaxacan moles. **Heat rating:** 1,500–2,500 Scoville units, mild.

SERRANO (*fresh*) → CHILE SECO (*dried*)

Serrano are sharper in flavor than a jalapeño, more grassy, less vegetal, and hotter than Mexican jalapeños. The chile seco has a red fruity sweet flavor, with nice heat. **Heat rating:** 10,000–23,000 Scoville units, boom.

CHILE DE ÁRBOL (*both fresh and dried*)

Super-spicy, bright flavor, slightly acidic. Similar to a Thai bird's eye chile. **Heat rating:** 15,000–30,000 Scoville units, fireworks in your mouth.

PEQUÍN (*both fresh and dried*)

Little round balls of fire. Slightly hotter than the cayenne, the pequín is loved by birds and is propagated by their poop (sorry, but it's true). Dried fruit flavor, with slight acidity. **Heat rating:** 30,000–60,000 Scoville units. Not for beginners.

CHILTEPÍN/CHILE TEPÍN (*fresh and dried*)

Small football- (American) shaped chiles with stone fruit notes and intensely hot, but the burn dissipates quickly. **Heat rating:** 100,000–200,000 Scoville units. Call 911!

HABANERO (*fresh*)

Citrusy tropical fruit flavor, hot hot hot! **Heat rating:** 100,000–350,000 Scoville units. Nirvana.

POBLANO

CHILE GUERO

JALAPEÑO

SERRANO

HABANERO

CHILHUACLE

DRIED
HABANERO

CHILE
DE ÁRBOL

MORITA

PEQUÍN

CHILTEPÍN

ANCHO

GUAJILLO

PASILLA

CHIPOTLE MECO

PUYA

CHILE SECO

SALSA TOOLS

Molcajete
A molcajete is a Mexican mortar and pestle. I love the tactile experience of smashing a salsa with a molcajete, as well as the nostalgia it brings me when I'm using the one my grandfather gave me when I moved to my first apartment. But truthfully, they've been usurped by electric blenders in most Mexican households. If you're interested in buying one, look for one from Mexico, of course. They're made from volcanic stone that's durable enough to last a lifetime.*

To season a molcajete, get some white rice and grind it to dust, ½ cup at a time. The first few cups might have flecks of stone in them, but like rinsing rice, keep grabbing a new handful and grinding until the powder is white and the molcajete is smooth—three to five rounds, depending on how rough it was—then brush the dust out and throw it in the dishwasher (don't tell anyone I told you). The process takes a while, so I recommend doing it on your front steps so you can meet all the neighbors and their nice dogs as they walk by. Mine is about 6 inches tall and 10 inches wide, with three little feet that help it stabilize on the counter.

*With normal usage. My mother used hers every day for 45 years, and one day when she asked me to grind some cumin, I broke it in half and started crying. She didn't flinch. She reached into the cabinet and pulled out another one like it was a paper towel.

Blender
I write about the universal love for the Oster blender on page 89, but for the purposes of this book, any blender will do the trick. (I have a Vitamix, but its ability to blend hard ingredients isn't really necessary in Salsa Land.) I even use a Magic Bullet for smaller portions of salsa when I want to whip something up fast and not have to wash the bulky Vitamix. A food processor will also work for blended salsas in this book though they might be a bit more chunky or coarse in texture. I would not recommend the food processor for moles.

Plastic cutting board
So many onions. So much garlic. So many chiles. The ingredients we're working with for salsas will leach their scent and soak their juices into a wooden cutting board (cleanable, but annoying), so I use a plastic cutting board exclusively for salsa along with an inexpensive, sharp knife (though not my beautiful Japanese knives, those are only used on wood). It's an OXO plastic board with a moat around

its perimeter, which keeps tomato juices from leaking all over the counter, and then I can pour those juices into my salsa. And it's dishwasher safe.

Foil + cast-iron skillet

Charring is a fundamental technique in Mexican cuisine that develops deeply savory and sweet notes. In the US, it can coax out the flavor of lackluster produce. My go-to method: Line a cast-iron skillet with a sheet of foil* to make sure no sticky tomato juices will seep through and char the pan, then heat it over high until it's ripping hot. Test with a flick of water—it should sizzle immediately and disappear. Note: This is a smoky process. Open your windows, turn on the vent, and disable the smoke alarms if you need to. Alternately, char your veg on the grill outside.

*PS: Sometimes I oil the cast iron before I lay the foil down to get a season session in. Multitask!

Broiler

If smoking up the kitchen isn't your scene—aww, no fun!—I recommend lining a sheet pan with foil, then broiling your vegetables. It'll take slightly longer than the stovetop method, but just keep an eye on things because the timing will depend on your oven.

Microplane

I use my microplane for garlic and citrus zest in salsas. There's a reason I call for grated garlic in my salsas as opposed to chopped, and that's because it causes the garlic to melt into the salsa and go on its merry way. Whereas when it's chopped, you get these little intense bites of garlic that can overpower your palate. I realize this is a pretty nuanced detail, so if you don't have a microplane or can't be bothered, just try to chop your garlic as finely as possible. For citrus, I find the zest in a salsa makes the citrus flavor pop more and last longer. But again, if you don't have a microplane, stick to the citrus juice.

Freeze your salsa!!

Almost every salsa in this book can freeze (and if not, it'll be noted). When you have salsa in the freezer, dinner can come together almost instantly (see Chapter 8 for recipes that show you how). Find the salsa that calls out to you, make it, and freeze half (or more) for later. I store mine in plastic deli containers, but you could do freezer bags too. To thaw, transfer it to the fridge the night before you need it. Who am I kidding. I never plan that far ahead. I usually thaw it in the microwave or leave it in the sink until dinnertime.

CAPSAICIN CORNER!

Capsaicin is the chemical compound that makes chiles spicy. It's especially concentrated in the white membrane inside chiles. Capsaicin increases blood flow, so you might also see it in the pharmacy as a pain-relieving agent for achy joints.

I love the fiery heat of chiles. It reminds me I'm alive. I didn't always used to be this way, though. As a kid, I avoided super-spicy food. But over time, the receptors on my tongue (these are different than taste buds, but let's not get too far in the weeds), got used to the heat and desensitized. That's how people adapt to spicy foods, and the burn of alcohol, for that matter. Worst-case scenario, you take on more heat than you can handle—the good news is, it only lasts around 15 minutes. Have a quesadilla and relax.

HOW TO TAME CHILES

For fresh and dried chiles, removing the chile's seeds will cut down on significant heat (the seeds don't contain capsaicin, but they do get coated in it) and move your salsa from hot to medium-spicy. If you're extra wary of spice, start with one chile for mild and work your way up. To almost completely remove a chile's heat and leave only its flavor, you can soak it. Capsaicin is soluble in alcohol, vinegar, and oil. That just means its spiciness will seep into the liquid around it, and it's a way of taking some of the heat out of the chile. (This is actually how Wilbur Scoville measured chile peppers' heat levels). Which method you use will depend on the salsa context.

ALCOHOL
Soak chopped chiles in a cup of alcohol (or more, for more chiles). In the Mermelada de Habaneros Celestial (page 118), I use tequila for flavor, but you could do any high-proof booze like Everclear or vodka*. The longer you leave the chile in alcohol, the tamer it'll become, but I find 45 minutes gets it done (and up to 3 hours if you must). To test your chile, pull a piece out, rinse it with water, and taste. I only use this method for chiles that'll get cooked into a salsa so it cooks off the alcohol and flavor.

This process does not make flavorful infused tequila. It makes liquid hellfire. You could keep it to make spicy margaritas a tiny teaspoon at a time, but I just toss it down the drain. It's also good for clogged drains.

VINEGAR
Ditto the alcohol method. But vinegar begins to pickle the chile. So in the Salsa Macha con Habaneros (page 205), it's awesome, because you want these juicy, sour, hot bites of chile.

OIL
Same method, but I never do this, because oil takes a lot longer to pull out the capsaicin.

TIME
Something wild happened in the making of this cookbook. I had to study the heat and flavor fluctuations in salsa in a way I never would as a home cook, but I wanted to be confident in how far ahead you could make salsas. I quickly learned that even the hottest of hot salsas were noticeably mellowed after 24 hours in the fridge.

FAT
That said, you're not always making a salsa 24 hours before you want to eat it. In that case, just add olive oil. Stir a tablespoon into your salsa until it's incorporated (and probably gives the salsa a nice sheen). My theory is that the oil's fat coats the tongue and dulls the heat, but the only proof I have is that when I add olive oil to super spicy salsas, it mellows out. Alternately, add a spoonful of crema, or blend in some avocado, to mute the chile's heat, depending on the flavor profile of the salsa.

REMOVE THE SEEDS
I have written these recipes the way I enjoy eating them: HOT! To tame the heat, you should carefully remove the seeds for medium, or use only one seedless chile for mild.

ADD MORE VEG
Adding more vegetables to your salsa is a great way to dilute the heat and use up what's sitting in the crisper drawer waiting for the compost bin. I often make a salsa with the random half-cucumbers, wrinkly stone fruit, and wilted lettuce in my fridge. Cucumber, sweet peppers, and any other vegetables or even tart grapes and berries can be added to any of the smashed, chopped, or blended salsas in Chapters 1 or 2. Lettuce usually adds some water and color but little flavor, so it can go in any of the blended salsas in Chapters 3.

SALSA ALCHEMY

I believe salsa belongs everywhere, all the time. In the salsa recipes that will follow (and in their photos; keep reading), I'll share lots of everyday ways to use them. Here are four go-to dishes I repeat when I'm swimming in leftover salsa.

Vegetable stock
Combine 1 cup salsa with 3 cups water to make 1 quart vegetable stock to use in soups and picadillo (see pages 268 and 252). Use salsas made with vegetables only (no meat, fruit, dairy or oil).

Fried rice
Heat a glug of olive oil or lard in a wok or nonstick skillet over high heat and cook your random greens or leftover protein and any other aromatics (separately), tossing constantly until the vegetables are crisp-tender. Next, add leftover rice, beaten egg, and more oil and cook, tossing constantly, until crisp and beginning to brown. Add anywhere from a few spoonfuls to ½ cup of salsa de mesa (save the hot sauce, pickles, and salsa macha for topping) along with a tablespoon or two of soy sauce and toss everything together until completely coated and all the liquid has evaporated.

Chicken dinner
Preheat the oven to 350°F. Season a whole chicken, chicken thighs, or breast (if you must) with salt, and then nestle into your favorite roasting pan. Pour at least 1 cup and up to 4 cups of leftover salsa over the chicken, and roast until the chicken is cooked through and an instant-read thermometer inserted into the thickest part of the thigh registers 165°F and the breast registers 145°F (the temp will continue to rise as it sits and cools). Seriously, that's it.

Poached shrimp
Heat 1 cup salsa and 1 cup water in a medium saucepan until simmering, then drop in 1 pound shrimp and cook until they turn opaque and pink, around 3 minutes. Also good with other creatures of the sea.

One last note before we jump in
You'll see a lot of non-Mexican food in the recipe photos. Because salsa goes with everything, no matter what culture or country it comes from. I believe it makes any food mind-blowingly delicious. So you'll see things like a tomato and tomatillo panzanella tossed in Salsa de Jamaica (page 133), and fried tofu triangles served over a bed of El Pepino (page 98) and Baile del Mango (page 78) tucked inside a pita stuffed with falafel. You already know these salsas will be great on a taco, but I want you to swirl a salsa into that buttery platter of shrimp scampi and realize that life will never be the same after this.

Taco rice bowl

1

SMASHED
SALSAS

MARTA

CHAPTER

MARTAJADAS
—SMASHED SALSAS

We're starting with the oldest way of making salsa: smashing it. You can use a molcajete, or a potato masher, or even your bare hands. Today in Mexico, everyone loves their blender. So for every recipe here, feel free to use one or a food processor if you want—I'll love you either way.

Salsas martajadas (smashed salsas) are more textured and give you a nice variation in flavor and texture, whether you spoon them over grilled meats or eat them with totopos (tortilla chips; see page 112 to make them yourself). Think: a sweet bite of tomato followed with a crisp, hot hit of chile serrano. So, if you do use a blender, just hold back on completely pulverizing the ingredients to preserve that chunky magic.

"Rick, why does every recipe . . .
. . . begin with charring or stewing the tomatoes, onion, and chile?" I do this to enhance their flavor and, more important, to soften them so they're easier to smash. That said, salsa is all about improv, flexibility, and doing what you damn well please. If you'd prefer to blend the ingredients raw, do it!

LA MAÑANERA

THE MORNING SALSA
Stewed tomato, tomatillo, onion, and chile de árbol

Mañanero in Mexico means "morning sex," which was my inspiration for this salsa, and so many other things in life. Sometimes you need a little something spicy to wake you up! This is my ideal Tex-Mex breakfast taco salsa; it's simple and fresh. The tomatillos bring acidity and brightness, so if you swap those for more tomatoes, I'd recommend a squeeze of lime to fill the missing beat. Also, there's no cilantro here, because it can be an assertive flavor and it's not legally required for every salsa, FYI. I'm making my own rules now, and I don't care who knows it.

MAKES 2 CUPS

- 2 medium Roma tomatoes (9.2 oz/ 261 g), cored and left whole
- 3 medium tomatillos (7.4 oz/211 g), husked and rinsed
- ¼ medium white onion (3.1 oz/89 g)
- 6 fresh or dried chiles de árbol (0.2 oz/6 g), stemmed and chopped
- 1 garlic clove, peeled but whole
- 1½ teaspoons Diamond Crystal kosher salt (0.21 oz/6 g), plus more to taste

SERVING SUGGESTIONS

All breakfast tacos and any food in need of a bright and spicy pick-me-up. This pairs very well with anything made of masa: tamales, Tostadas (page 113), tacos, huaraches. Also a great way to zhuzh up canned beans—or use in cooking broth!

1. In a medium saucepan, combine ½ cup water, the tomatoes, tomatillos, onion, and chiles de árbol and bring to a boil over high heat. Cover, reduce to a simmer, and cook until the tomatoes have softened and are just holding their shape, about 10 minutes. Transfer the vegetables to a plate to cool and reserve the cooking liquid.

2. Working in batches, use a molcajete or mortar and pestle (or a medium bowl with a potato masher, large spoon, or forks) to smash and grind the tomatoes, tomatillos, onion, chiles de árbol, and garlic until a chunky but pourable salsa forms; thin the salsa with cooking liquid if desired. (Alternatively, use a blender and purée on low speed until the salsa is almost smooth but some pieces remain.) Transfer to a medium bowl and stir in the salt. Taste and season with more salt if desired.

Do ahead: The salsa can be made up to 2 days ahead. Store in an airtight container in the refrigerator, or freeze for up to 1 month.

SWAP CORNER
Can't find tomatillos where you are? Use more tomatoes and a tablespoon of lime juice; they should total 1 pound.

RICK'S
BREAKFAST
TACOS
PAGE 224

Carne asada, shrimp, nopales, spring onions, and zucchini

LA MOLCAJETEADA

MOLCAJETE-MADE SALSA
Charred tomato, onion, serrano, and jalapeño

This is my salsa tatemada, a chunky, charred tomato taqueria salsa that'll convince you to never buy it jarred again. I named it molcajeteada to reference the tool it's made in. When I was twenty-two, my grandfather gave me my first molcajete—and a bag of rice. "What's this for?" I asked, and he told me I had to grind it into the molcajete to smooth out the gritty volcanic rock. I was so mad. *Can't you just buy one already seasoned?* my entitled, youthful self thought. But later, there I was, grinding that rice until my molcajete was glassy smooth. Anyway, you can use a blender—I'm using my hand-seasoned molcajete.

MAKES 2 CUPS

- 4 medium Roma tomatoes or tomatillos (1 lb/453 g), cored and left whole
- ¼ medium white onion (3.1 oz/89 g)
- 2 chiles serranos (1.3 oz/38 g), stemmed
- 1 chile jalapeño (1 oz/31 g), stemmed
- 2 garlic cloves, unpeeled
- 1 tablespoon chopped fresh cilantro leaves with tender stems (0.14 oz/4 g)
- 1 tablespoon fresh lime juice, plus more to taste
- 1½ teaspoons Diamond Crystal kosher salt (0.21 oz/6 g), plus more to taste

SERVING SUGGESTIONS

Great with anything grilled, anything inside a taco, fried seafood, and even raw vegetables. Use anywhere you would ketchup, if you're into a little kick.

1. Line a large cast-iron skillet with a sheet of foil and heat the skillet over high until very hot. Add the tomatoes, onion, serranos, jalapeño, and garlic and cook, using tongs to turn occasionally, until everything is charred on all sides, about 3 minutes for the garlic, 4 to 5 minutes for the chiles, 6 to 8 minutes for the onion, and 8 to 10 minutes for the tomatoes. (Alternatively, arrange an oven rack in the top position and preheat the broiler to high. Arrange the vegetables on a foil-lined sheet pan and roast under the broiler, turning occasionally, until all sides are charred.) Transfer to a plate to cool. Once cool enough to handle, peel the garlic.

2. Working in batches, use a molcajete or mortar and pestle (or a medium bowl with a potato masher, large spoon, or forks) to smash and grind the tomatoes, onion, serranos, jalapeño, and garlic until a chunky but pourable salsa forms. (Alternatively, use a blender and purée on low speed until the salsa is almost smooth but some pieces remain.)

3. Transfer to a medium bowl and stir in the cilantro, lime juice, and salt. Taste and season with more salt and lime juice if desired.

Do ahead: The salsa can be made up to 2 days ahead. Store in an airtight container in the refrigerator, or freeze for up to 1 month.

LA TATEMADA CREMOSA

CHARRED AND CREAMY
Charred tomato, chipotle in adobo, and crema

This is a smoky and creamy variation on salsa tatemada (see Molcajeteada, page 35), but using canned chipotles in adobo sauce instead of fresh chiles, and two spoonfuls of crema because I'm a lush for cultured dairy. It's an anywhere, anytime salsa that's especially friendly to grilled meats, pulled chicken (like the Tostadas de Tinga de Pollo on page 250), and veggies. I can't wrap my head around how good this salsa is. Well, yes, I can. It's the crema. Just make it!

MAKES 2 CUPS

- 3 medium Roma tomatoes (12 oz/342 g), cored and left whole
- ¼ medium white onion (3.1 oz/89 g)
- 1 garlic clove, unpeeled
- 3 chipotle chiles in adobo
- 1 tablespoon adobo sauce
- 2 tablespoons crema, crème fraîche, or sour cream
- 1½ teaspoons Diamond Crystal kosher salt (0.21 oz/6 g), plus more to taste

SERVING SUGGESTIONS

Definitely with chips. Hot dogs, burgers, and sandwiches. Stir into cream or cheese sauces or serve like gravy, alongside fried chicken or over a chicken fried steak.

1. Line a large cast-iron skillet with a sheet of foil and heat the skillet over high until very hot. Add the tomatoes, onion, and garlic and cook, using tongs to turn occasionally, until everything is charred on all sides, about 3 minutes for the garlic, 6 to 8 minutes for the onion, and 8 to 10 minutes for the tomatoes. (Alternatively, arrange an oven rack in the top position and preheat the broiler to high. Arrange the vegetables on a foil-lined sheet pan and roast under the broiler, turning occasionally, until all sides are charred.) Transfer to a plate to cool. Once cool enough to handle, peel the garlic.

2. Working in batches, use a molcajete or mortar and pestle (or a medium bowl with a potato masher, large spoon, or forks) to smash and grind the tomatoes, onion, garlic, and chiles until a chunky but pourable salsa forms. (Alternatively, use a blender and purée on low speed until the salsa is almost smooth but some pieces remain.)

3. Transfer to a medium bowl and stir in the adobo sauce, crema, and salt. Taste and season with more salt if desired.

Do ahead: The salsa can be made up to 2 days ahead. Store in an airtight container in the refrigerator, or freeze for up to 1 month.

SWAP CORNER
Scared of a little spice? Shhh . . . everything's going to be okay. Use just the adobo sauce from the chipotle chiles and you'll get that deep, smoky flavor with a much tamer heat. Or add more crema. Can't hurt.

Shish Tawook
(Chicken skewers)

Ribeye steak sandwich with focaccia

LA VERDE CREMOSA

CREAMY GREEN
Charred tomatillo and serrano,
with smashed avocado

This salsa is all about the hunks—words to live by. Tomatillo and avocado are so good together because the tomatillo's sharpness cuts through the avocado's richness. There's some heat here, but the hunks of avocado balance it in a beautiful dance. As I went back for another scoop and another scoop, I realized this would be incredible on a steak sandwich. But by the next scoop, it was gone.

MAKES 2 CUPS

- 4 medium tomatillos (8.4 oz/240 g), husked and rinsed
- ¼ medium white onion (3.1 oz/89 g)
- 2 chiles serranos (1 oz/30 g), stemmed
- 1 garlic clove, peeled
- 1 medium avocado (6 oz/170 g), peeled and seeded
- 1½ teaspoons Diamond Crystal kosher salt (0.21 oz/6 g), plus more to taste

SERVING SUGGESTIONS

Grilled corn, grilled seafood, fried eggs, rice bowls, and salads.

1. Line a large cast-iron skillet with a sheet of foil and heat the skillet over high until very hot. Add the tomatillos, onion, and serranos and cook, using tongs to turn occasionally, until everything is charred on all sides, 4 to 5 minutes for the chiles, 6 to 8 minutes for the onion, and 8 to 10 minutes for the tomatillos. (Alternatively, arrange an oven rack in the top position and preheat the broiler to high. Arrange the vegetables on a foil-lined sheet pan and roast under the broiler, turning occasionally, until all sides are charred.) Transfer to a plate to cool.

2. Working in batches and using a molcajete or mortar and pestle (or a medium bowl with a potato masher, large spoon, or forks), smash and grind the tomatillos, onion, serranos, garlic, and avocado until a chunky but pourable salsa forms. (Alternatively, use a blender and purée everything but the avocado on low speed until the salsa is almost smooth but some pieces remain. Smash the avocado separately with a fork and stir into the blended salsa.)

3. Transfer to a medium bowl and stir in the salt. Taste and season with more salt if desired.

Do ahead: The salsa can be made up to 2 days ahead. Store in an airtight container in the refrigerator.

LA PEPITA ROJA

THE RED PUMPKIN SEED
Charred tomato and habanero
with crushed pumpkin seeds

The crispy bits of crushed toasted pepitas (aka pumpkin seeds) are irresistible in this salsa, inspired by Ha' Sikil P'ak, a Mayan dip you can find a recipe for in *Mi Cocina*. Here the texture is less of a creamy dip and more of a loose, nutty salsa. I use a blend of orange and lime zest to re-create the flavor of sour oranges from the Yucatán, and that citrus sweetness explodes against the smoky tomato and hot habanero in a sultry, delectable way, especially when it's paired with fresh seafood.

MAKES 2 CUPS

- 4 medium Roma tomatoes (1 lb/453 g), cored and left whole
- ¼ medium white onion (3.1 oz/89 g)
- 1 chile habanero (0.3 oz/10 g), stemmed
- 2 garlic cloves, unpeeled
- ½ cup pepitas/raw pumpkin seeds (2 oz/56 g)
- ¼ cup fresh orange juice, plus more to taste
- ½ teaspoon finely grated orange zest
- ½ teaspoon finely grated lime zest
- 1½ teaspoons Diamond Crystal kosher salt (0.21 oz/6 g), plus more to taste

SERVING SUGGESTIONS

Fried or roasted plantains; baked potatoes; dressing for grain bowls; raw, steamed, baked, or poached seafood.

1. Line a large cast-iron skillet with a sheet of foil and heat the skillet over high until very hot. Add the tomatoes, onion, habanero, and garlic and cook, using tongs to turn occasionally, until everything is charred on all sides, about 3 minutes for the garlic, 4 to 5 minutes for the chile, 6 to 8 minutes for the onion, and 8 to 10 minutes for the tomatoes. (Alternatively, arrange an oven rack in the top position and preheat the broiler to high. Arrange the vegetables on a sheet pan lined with foil and roast under the broiler, turning occasionally, until all sides are charred.) Transfer to a plate to cool. Once cool enough to handle, peel the garlic.

2. Let the skillet cool slightly, carefully remove the foil, and reduce the heat to medium. Add the pumpkin seeds and toast, tossing frequently, until very fragrant and browned and beginning to pop, 3 to 4 minutes. Transfer to a molcajete or mortar and pestle and crush the pepitas until almost finely ground, but you want a few larger pieces for added texture. (Alternatively, finely chop the pepitas by hand.) Transfer to a medium bowl.

3. Working in batches, use a molcajete or mortar and pestle (or a medium bowl with a potato masher, large spoon, or forks) to smash and grind the tomatoes, onion, habanero, and garlic until a chunky but pourable salsa forms. (Alternatively, use a blender and purée on low speed until the salsa is almost smooth but some pieces remain.)

4. Transfer the salsa to the bowl with the crushed pepitas and stir in the orange juice, orange zest, lime zest, and salt. Taste and season with more orange juice and salt if desired.

Do ahead: The salsa can be made up to 2 days ahead. Store in an airtight container in the refrigerator, or freeze for up to 1 month.

Fried plantains, totopos, chicharrones, and veggies

Scallop ceviche

CHILE FRESCO Y CÍTRICO

CITRUSY FRESH CHILES
Charred fresh güeros with orange and lime

Here's proof that salsa doesn't always need tomatoes or tomatillos as a base. This salsa stars chiles güeros, slightly sweet and not-very-spicy yellow chiles, which are used commonly along the Gulf coast in Mexico. If you can't get them, other mostly sweet yellow peppers, such as banana, wax, or bells will work. The güeros in this salsa are charred and caramelly, but the tang of the lime and sweetness of the orange gives them a bright, summery finish. I love it with grilled seafood or a charred steak. Or mix it into some mayonnaise and slather it over your favorite burger.

MAKES 1½ CUPS

- 4 large fresh yellow chiles güeros/caribes (10 oz/282 g), banana, wax, or yellow bell peppers, stemmed
- 1 chile serrano (0.7 oz/20 g), stemmed
- ¼ medium white onion (3.1 oz/89 g)
- 1 garlic clove, unpeeled
- ¼ cup fresh orange juice
- 1 tablespoon fresh lime juice
- ½ teaspoon finely grated orange zest
- ½ teaspoon finely grated lime zest
- 1 chile de árbol (0.03 oz/1 g), stemmed and chopped
- 1½ teaspoons Diamond Crystal kosher salt (0.21 oz/6 g), plus more to taste

SERVING SUGGESTIONS

Pour over raw seafood and let it sit for 5 minutes for an amazing ceviche. Use as a sauce for grilled meats or veggies. Mix into mayonnaise and use on sandwiches or stir into sour cream for a punchy dip.

1. Line a large cast-iron skillet with a sheet of foil and heat the skillet over high until very hot. Add the güeros, serrano, onion, and garlic and cook, using tongs to turn occasionally, until everything is charred on all sides, about 3 minutes for the garlic, 4 to 5 minutes for the chiles, 6 to 8 minutes for the onion, and 8 to 10 minutes for the tomatoes. Transfer to a plate to cool. (Alternatively, arrange an oven rack in the top position and preheat the broiler to high. Arrange the vegetables on a foil-lined sheet pan and roast under the broiler, turning occasionally, until all sides are charred.) Once cool enough to handle, peel the garlic (and remove the seeds if using bell peppers).

2. Working in batches, use a molcajete or mortar and pestle (or a medium bowl with a potato masher, large spoon, or forks) to smash and grind the güeros, serrano, onion, and peeled garlic until a chunky salsa forms. (Alternatively, use a blender and purée on low speed until the salsa is almost smooth but some pieces remain.)

3. Transfer to a medium bowl and stir in the orange juice, lime juice, orange zest, lime zest, chile de árbol, and salt. Taste and season with more salt if desired.

Do ahead: The salsa can be made up to 2 days ahead. Store in an airtight container in the refrigerator, or freeze for up to 1 month.

LA PIÑA

THE PINEAPPLE
Charred pineapple and habanero
with a drizzle of olive oil

This salsa is sweet, tangy, tropical, and delicious, just
how I like it, with a simple ingredient list centered around
my love of pineapple. There's a finishing touch—a drizzle
of olive oil. I added it on a whim, but the oil's grassiness
deepened the flavors so it tasted like it had cooked
a lot longer than it had, while also creating a creamy,
emulsified texture. We all have a calling, and this special
salsa was born to be with Camarones al Coco (page 276).

MAKES 1½ CUPS

- ½ medium pineapple (1 lb/460 g), peeled, cored, and thinly sliced
- 3 tablespoons extra-virgin olive oil, divided
- ¼ medium white onion (3.1 oz/89 g)
- 2 chiles habaneros (0.7 oz/22 g), stemmed, halved, and seeded
- 2 garlic cloves, unpeeled
- 1½ teaspoons Diamond Crystal kosher salt (0.21 oz/6 g), plus more to taste

SERVING SUGGESTIONS

Shrimp! All seafood. Or with chips, at the
beach or pool.

1. Brush both sides of the pineapple with 1 tablespoon
of the olive oil to prevent them from sticking.

2. Line a large cast-iron skillet with a sheet of foil and heat
the skillet over high heat (and I mean high, we need that
pineapple to caramelize, not steam) until very hot. Working
in batches, add the pineapple, onion, habaneros, and garlic
and cook, using tongs to turn occasionally, until everything
is charred on all sides, about 3 minutes for the garlic, 3 to
4 minutes for the chiles, and 6 to 8 minutes for the onion
and pineapple. (Alternatively, arrange an oven rack in the
top position and preheat the broiler to high. Arrange the
pineapple and vegetables on a foil-lined sheet pan and
roast under the broiler, turning occasionally, until all sides
are charred.) Transfer to a plate to cool.

3. Working in batches, use a molcajete or mortar and
pestle to smash and grind the pineapple, onion, habaneros,
and garlic until a chunky but pourable salsa forms.

4. Transfer to a medium bowl and stir in the remaining
2 tablespoons olive oil and the salt. Taste and season with
more salt if desired.

Do ahead: The salsa can be made up to 2 days ahead.
Store in an airtight container in the refrigerator, or freeze for
up to 1 month.

WORK WITH THE PINEAPPLE YOU'VE GOT
Ideally, you're using a sweet, ripe pineapple with a hint of give
when you press into its spiky skin. If your pineapple is on the
underripe, greener side, char it and then blend it, because it'll be
too firm to easily smash, and the heat will caramelize the sugar
and make it taste sweeter than it actually is.

CAMARONES
AL COCO
PAGE 276

Crudités platter

LA HABA FRESCA

THE FRESH FAVA
Stewed tomatillo, jalapeño, and fresh favas

We've been in Salsa Land for a few pages here already, but this lively fava salsa pushes us in a new direction with a springy green flavor and a hearty, bejeweled texture that you can scoop up or toss into salads. In central Mexico, fava beans are as much a part of daily eating life as black beans, whereas when I lived in New York, they were a precious springtime gem. You can serve this on a crudités platter, with grilled (vegan or pork) chorizo and crisp-fresh endive, or just demolish it with saltines, like I did.

MAKES 2 CUPS

- 4 medium tomatillos (8.8 oz/250 g), husked and rinsed
- ¼ medium white onion (3.1 oz/89 g)
- 2 chiles jalapeños (2.2 oz/62 g), stemmed
- 1 garlic clove, peeled but whole
- 1⅓ cups shelled fava beans (6 oz/170 g), fresh or thawed frozen
- 2 tablespoons chopped fresh mint leaves (0.28 oz/8 g)
- 1½ teaspoons Diamond Crystal kosher salt (0.21 oz/6 g), plus more to taste

SERVING SUGGESTIONS

Perfect with raw, roasted, fried, or grilled vegetables. Amazing with cheese, like a grilled cheese sandwich, Tex-Mex enchiladas (page 234), or a quesadilla (page 263). Or as a dip with pita chips or crackers.

1. In a medium saucepan, combine ½ cup water, the tomatillos, onion, jalapeños, and garlic and bring to a boil. Cover, reduce to a simmer, and cook until the tomatillos have softened and are just holding their shape, about 10 minutes. Transfer to a plate to cool and reserve the cooking liquid.

2. Working in batches, use a molcajete or mortar and pestle (or a medium bowl with a potato masher, large spoon, or forks) to smash and grind the tomatillos, onion, jalapeños, garlic, and fava beans until a chunky but pourable salsa forms; thin the salsa with a little of the cooking liquid if desired. (Alternatively, use a blender and purée on low speed until the salsa is almost smooth but some pieces remain.)

3. Transfer to a medium bowl and stir in the mint and salt. Taste and season with more salt if desired. The fava beans will absorb liquid as they sit, so use the reserved cooking liquid to thin the salsa before serving.

Do ahead: The salsa can be made up to 2 days ahead. Store in an airtight container in the refrigerator, or freeze for up to 1 month.

SWAP CORNER
Don't have access to fresh or frozen fava beans? Give peas a chance!

LA CIRUELA AGRIDULCE

THE SWEET AND SOUR PLUM
Jammy-tart plums, Fresno chiles, garlic, and lime

I used to make this salsa when I was cooking for a beach house full of extremely attractive men on Fire Island (tough life). It always caught them by surprise, which, in a house full of guys in glittery speedos, is hard to do. But the lesson here is to put fruit in your salsas. The juicy plums will soak up the chile and garlic before it gets too sweet (it won't be). Don't bother with peeling the plums, it'll all blend up just fine, and the sooner you're serving salsa and chips by the pool, the better.

MAKES 1½ CUPS

- 6 large ripe red or black plums (1 lb/460 g), stemmed
- 1 Fresno chile (2.4 oz/70 g), stemmed
- 1 garlic clove, peeled but whole
- 1 tablespoon chopped fresh basil leaves (0.14 oz/4 g)
- 1 tablespoon fresh lime juice
- 1 teaspoon grated lime zest
- 1½ teaspoons Diamond Crystal kosher salt (0.21 oz/6 g), plus more to taste

SERVING SUGGESTIONS

Fried, rich or heavy foods in need of a hit of fruity sweet and tart. It's great over roast pork or roast beef, with brisket, or Thanksgiving turkey.

1. In a medium saucepan, combine ½ cup water, the plums, Fresno chile, and garlic and bring to a boil. Cover, reduce to a simmer, and cook until the plums have softened and are just holding their shape, about 10 minutes. Transfer to a plate to cool and reserve the cooking liquid. When cool enough to handle, cut the plums in half and pit them.

2. Working in batches, use a molcajete or mortar and pestle (or a medium bowl with a potato masher, large spoon, or forks) to smash and grind the plums (skins, too!), chile, and garlic until a jammy salsa forms; thin the salsa with a little of the cooking liquid if desired. (Alternatively, use a blender and purée on low speed until the salsa is almost smooth but some pieces remain.)

3. Transfer to a medium bowl and stir in the basil, lime juice, lime zest, and salt and stir to combine. Taste and season with more salt if desired.

Do ahead: The salsa can be made up to 2 days ahead. Store in an airtight container in the refrigerator, or freeze for up to 1 month.

SWAP CORNER
Cilantro, I love you, but you're not the only herb in the world. You can use mint, lemon basil, shiso, lemon balm, or any favorite tender summer herb in this recipe and trust me, the men in glitter will adore it.

Pan roasted pork
chops and potatoes

QUESADILLAS
LAS MEJORES
PAGE 263

LA BORRACHA

DRUNKEN SALSA
Charred tomato, tomatillo, serrano, and jalapeño simmered in beer

This is a classic salsa, sometimes made with pulque (fermented drink made from the sap of maguey/agave plants), tequila, or mezcal, but I prefer it with a light Mexican lager like Pacífico. When the beer cooks down, the essence of malted barley and spicy hops remains and pairs perfectly with anything on the grill. Like any salsa, I've had my way with it to make it my own, and you should, too. My best decision? Adding a teaspoon of chicken bouillon powder. That makes everything better (read about it on page 14). As a result, this salsa is ridiculously hard to stop scooping into.

MAKES 1½ CUPS

- 2 **medium Roma tomatoes (½ lb/226 g), cored and left whole**
- 2 **medium tomatillos (4.2 oz/120 g), husked and rinsed**
- ¼ **medium white onion (3.1 oz/89 g)**
- 1 **chile serrano (0.7 oz/20 g), stemmed**
- 2 **chiles jalapeños (2.8 oz/80 g), stemmed**
- 2 **garlic cloves, unpeeled**
- 1 **tablespoon extra-virgin olive oil**
- ½ **cup pale lager, preferably Mexican**
- 1 **teaspoon Diamond Crystal kosher salt (0.14 oz/4 g), plus more to taste**
- 1 **teaspoon chicken bouillon powder (optional; see page 14)**

SERVING SUGGESTIONS

A bottle of beer and bar snacks. Tex-Mex. Tacos, rice, beans, Tostadas (page 113), tortas, Totopos (page 112).

1. Line a large cast-iron skillet with a sheet of foil and heat the skillet over high until very hot. Add the tomatoes, tomatillos, onion, serrano, jalapeños, and garlic and cook, using tongs to turn occasionally, until everything is charred on all sides, about 3 minutes for the garlic, 4 to 5 minutes for the chiles, 6 to 8 minutes for the onion, and 8 to 10 minutes for the tomatoes and tomatillos. (Alternatively, arrange an oven rack in the top position and preheat the broiler to high. Arrange the vegetables on a foil-lined sheet pan and roast under the broiler, turning occasionally, until all sides are charred.) Transfer to a plate to cool. Once cool enough to handle, peel the garlic.

2. Working in batches, use a molcajete or mortar and pestle (or a medium bowl with a potato masher, large spoon, or forks) to smash and grind the tomatoes, tomatillos, onion, serrano, jalapeños, and peeled garlic until a chunky but pourable salsa forms. (Alternatively, use a blender and purée on low speed until the salsa is almost smooth but some pieces remain.)

3. Remove the foil from the skillet, set it over high, and heat the oil until it is very hot. Carefully pour the salsa into the hot oil; it will spit and sputter, so wear an apron. Stir, scraping up any stuck-on bits from the bottom of the skillet and cook until most of the liquid has evaporated and the salsa looks like a chunky pasta sauce, about 2 minutes. Stir in the beer, salt, and bouillon powder (if using) and continue to cook until most of the liquid has evaporated and the smell of raw alcohol is gone, about 5 minutes. Taste and season with more salt if desired.

Do ahead: The salsa can be made up to 2 days ahead. Store in an airtight container in the refrigerator, or freeze for up to 1 month.

SALSAS FROM HOME

My mother, Gloria, was a fantastic cook, and my father, Richard, is also a fantastic cook, and they each had their own signature salsas made with tomatoes, chiles, and herbs from our backyard garden. When I was a kid, we called salsa "chile," and it was always on the table for any food that needed a drop of moisture and a smack of spice, from hot dogs to fried chicken. When I saw my mom's chile pot—a small stainless steel pot with a black handle—on the stove, and I could smell the tomatoes and chiles bubbling, I knew a salsa was coming. She changed it up with fresh-picked jalapeño or chile pequín one week, then dried the next, but there was always a jar of it in the fridge. I didn't eat much of it as a kid because I didn't have a taste for heat yet. But when I was in college, my mother would make elaborate breakfast spreads for me and my hungover friends that became legendary—crispy fried potatoes, smothered chicharrones, homemade chorizo, bacon-y refried beans, perfectly scrambled eggs, and fresh flour tortillas—and suddenly I began to appreciate that spicy salsa. Deeply. Soon I began to realize that no party was as good as my mom's breakfast the day after.

After my mother died in 2011, my father carried on the salsa torch. And I suppose I did, too, with this book. This recipe for my dad's salsa is a new invention. I was staying with him in Austin recently and when he handed me a plate of breakfast tacos (I am very blessed), he pointed to his salsa and said, "Watch out, this one's really hot." He'd run out of tomatoes and improvised with an all-jalapeño salsa doused with his Costco-size barrel of garlic powder he was trying to use up. It was amazing. As the salsa sat, the flavors melded and the garlic powder deepened and got almost toasty in a way raw garlic never would. I was blown away. And yes, it is very hot.

MOM'S SALSA DE MESA

Stewed tomato, pequín, and garlic

MAKES 1½ CUPS

- 4   medium Roma tomatoes (15.9 oz/452 g), cored and left whole
- 16 fresh or dried, red or green, chiles pequínes (0.1 oz/3 g), stemmed
- 1   garlic clove, peeled but whole
- 1½ teaspoons Diamond Crystal kosher salt (0.21 oz/6 g), plus more to taste

1. In a medium saucepan, combine ½ cup water and the tomatoes and bring to a boil over high heat. Cover, reduce to a simmer, and cook until the tomatoes have softened and are just holding their shape, about 10 minutes. Transfer to a plate to cool and reserve the cooking liquid.

2. Working in batches, use a molcajete or mortar and pestle (or a medium bowl with a potato masher, large spoon, or forks) to smash and grind the tomatoes, chiles pequínes, and garlic until a chunky but pourable salsa forms; thin the salsa with a little of the cooking liquid if desired. (Alternatively, use a blender and purée on low speed until the salsa is almost smooth but some pieces remain.)

3. Transfer to a medium bowl and stir in the salt. Taste and season with more salt if desired.

Do ahead: The salsa can be made up to 2 days ahead. Store in an airtight container in the refrigerator, or freeze for up to 1 month.

Bacon and refried bean taco

DADDY'S PURE JALAPEÑO SALSA

Stewed jalapeños and
garlic powder

MAKES 1 CUP

- 4   chiles jalapeños (6.1 oz/175 g),
  stemmed
- 1½ teaspoons garlic powder
- 1   teaspoon Diamond Crystal kosher
  salt (0.14 oz/4 g), plus more to taste

1. In a medium saucepan, combine ½ cup water and the jalapeños and bring to a boil over high heat. Cover, reduce to a simmer, and cook until the jalapeños have softened and are just holding their shape, about 10 minutes. Transfer to a plate to cool and reserve the cooking liquid.

2. Working in batches, use a molcajete or mortar and pestle (or a medium bowl with a potato masher, large spoon, or forks) to smash and grind the jalapeños until a chunky paste forms. (Alternatively, use a blender and purée on low speed until the salsa is almost smooth but some pieces remain.)

3. Transfer to a medium bowl and stir in ¼ cup of the cooking liquid, the garlic powder, and salt. Taste and season with more salt if desired.

Do ahead: The salsa can be made up to 2 days ahead. Store in an airtight container in the refrigerator, or freeze for up to 1 month.

P.S.
Hear me out. I like this salsa much more after a quick ferment on the counter for 3 to 4 days, depending on how warm your house is. (Don't tell my dad!) The ferment mellows the heat of the jalapeños and brings a hint, just a hint, of acidity. Then I spoon the salsa on pizza or anywhere you'd use a pickled jalapeño.

2.

CHOPPED
SALSAS

PICA

2

PICADAS
—CHOPPED SALSAS

I love a pico de gallo on a big Tex-Mex platter of smothered enchiladas, but picos de gallo are not always tomato, onion, and jalapeño. They're a whole category of chopped salsas, salads, and snacks made with different fruits, vegetables, nuts, and seeds. They can be made raw or charred, cooked and then chopped. Picos bring a pop of freshness and texture to anything that might be stewed, creamy, or fried. Because they aren't as liquidy as blended or smashed salsas, I like using them on tacos and tortas with saucy fillings or a steamy guiso (stew) like my mom's Chile Colorado (see page 264). Some of these picos are so good, you'll just want to eat them straight out of the bowl like I did—with no chips and no tacos. All you need is a spoon. (See Baile del Mango, page 78.)

Jícama, cucumber, xoconostle (sour prickly pear), guajes (a seed from a mimosoid tree native to southern Mexico), and oranges are commonly used in picos de gallo across Mexico, but I use red plums in place of the prickly pear and pepitas for the guajes when I'm in the US. Have you ever tried looking for a fresh ripe prickly pear in New York City?

But you should play with whatever's local, in season, and delicious to you. Be free! In these recipes, I keep it simple with raw ingredients you chop, stir, and eat, but if you want to try them charred, go for it. If you want to use watermelon instead of jícama, do it. There are no salsa police!

A Food Styling Trick
Listen, you chop however you want to chop. But in my years of food styling, I learned to vary the cut size of each ingredient, making the largest cut with the prettiest, most colorful ingredient so that it stands out in the crowd. The onion and the chiles usually get a medium cut, while the herbs get a super-fine chop until all you see is green confetti.

PICO DE GALLO CLÁSICO O SALSA MEXICANA

Tomato, onion, and jalapeño

While it's also called salsa Mexicana because of the green, white, and red hues, this classic pico always reminds me of home in Texas. My mom would fry tostadas and top them with bacon-y refried beans, melted cheddar cheese, and juicy links of smoked Elgin sausage (a specialty from Elgin, Texas). It was a sin to eat the tostada without pico de gallo. You needed to balance the tostada's crunch with tomato juices dripping down your chin, as the lord intended.

MAKES 2 CUPS

- 2 medium Roma tomatoes (8.6 oz/246 g), chopped
- ¼ medium white onion (3.1 oz/89 g), chopped
- 2 chiles jalapeños (2.2 oz/62 g), stemmed and chopped
- 1 garlic clove, grated
- 2 tablespoons chopped fresh cilantro leaves with tender stems (0.28 oz/8 g)
- 2 tablespoons fresh lime juice
- 1¼ teaspoons Diamond Crystal kosher salt (0.17 oz/5 g), plus more to taste

SERVING SUGGESTIONS

Spoon over enchiladas or Picadillo de Chorizo y Camarones (page 255); serve as a side to roasted fish; add to tortas or sandwiches like you would tomato and onion; garnish nachos and tostadas, and whatever else strikes your fancy.

In a medium bowl, gently stir together the tomatoes, onion, jalapeños, garlic, cilantro, lime juice, and salt until completely combined. Taste and season with more salt and lime juice if desired. Let sit, uncovered, for about 10 minutes so the flavors can meld.

Do ahead: The salsa can be made up to 1 day ahead. Store in an airtight container in the refrigerator.

WHAT MAKES A BAD PICO DE GALLO?
Mealy tomatoes. Overdoing it on cilantro (it can happen!). Skimping on jalapeños so the tomatoes have no counterbalance. But the biggest mistake would be not making it in the first place.

Huaraches
with nopal salad

Fried fish fillet

BESITOS DE KIWI

KIWI KISSES
Kiwi, tomatillo, and serrano

This gorgeous green salsa not only tastes like a day at the beach, but it begs for food you'd find there, like fried fish tacos. We're using one of my favorite combinations, tomatillo and kiwi, a deeply underrated duo. The kiwi functions similarly to tomato (soft, sweet, juicy), but its tropical flavor matches up with the tangy tomatillo in a way that makes them both brighter and bigger. A bit of basil always transports me to summer. And it's not as sweet as you might expect, thanks to the spicy serranos.

MAKES 2 CUPS

- 4 medium tomatillos (8.4 oz/240 g), husked, rinsed, and chopped
- 3 medium kiwis (8.8 oz/251 g), peeled and chopped
- ¼ medium red onion (3.1 oz/89 g), chopped
- 3 chiles serranos (1.6 oz/45 g), stemmed and chopped
- 1 garlic clove, grated
- 2 tablespoons chopped fresh basil (0.28 oz/8 g) or mint/lemon balm
- 2 tablespoons fresh lime juice, plus more to taste
- 1½ teaspoons Diamond Crystal kosher salt (0.21 oz/6 g), plus more to taste

SERVING SUGGESTIONS

Any and all seafood—Camarones al Coco (Coconut Shrimp, page 276), raw oysters, ceviche—vegetable carpaccio or even birria, carnitas, or grits: anything soft that needs some texture.

In a medium bowl, gently stir together the tomatillos, kiwis, onion, serranos, garlic, basil, lime juice, and salt until completely combined. Taste and season with more salt and lime juice if desired. Let sit, uncovered, for about 10 minutes so the flavors can meld.

Do ahead: The salsa can be made up to 1 day ahead. Store in an airtight container in the refrigerator.

WHY ARE WE GRATING THE GARLIC?
Grating makes the garlic "melt" into the salsa so you don't get bites of hot, raw garlic that ruin your day.

XNIPEC

YUCATECAN SALSA
Tomato, habanero,
and sour orange

Xnipec (pronounced shnee-pic) means "dog's nose,"
so named because the habaneros are so hot, they'll make
your nose run, like a dog's wet nose. But don't worry, in
my version of this iconic salsa, we take the seeds out of
the habaneros and add tomato to tame the heat. The fruity
habaneros and sweet orange juice always take me to the
Yucatán, and so I crave this salsa with dishes from that
region, like cochinita pibil (check the recipe in *Mi Cocina*).
If you've already made the classic pico de gallo in this
chapter and want to up your game, make this next. You
might never go back.

MAKES 2 CUPS

- 2 medium Roma tomatoes
  (8.6 oz/246 g), chopped

- ¼ medium red onion (3.1 oz/89 g),
  chopped

- 2 chiles habaneros (0.7 oz/22 g),
  stemmed, seeded, and chopped

- ¼ cup chopped fresh cilantro leaves
  with tender stems (0.56 oz/16 g)

- 2 tablespoons fresh lime juice, plus
  more to taste

- 2 tablespoons fresh orange juice

- 1 teaspoon Diamond Crystal kosher
  salt (0.14 oz/4 g), plus more to taste

SERVING SUGGESTIONS

Cochinita pibil, barbacoa, or anywhere
you'd use a classic pico but crave more
heat and sweetness.

In a medium bowl, gently stir together the tomatoes, onion,
habaneros, cilantro, lime juice, orange juice, and salt until
completely combined. Taste and season with more salt and
lime juice if desired. Let sit, uncovered, for about 10 minutes
so the flavors can meld.

Do ahead: The salsa can be made up to 1 day ahead (and
that will mellow its heat). Store in an airtight container in
the refrigerator.

Salbutes with cochinita pibil

Totopos and tequila

CIRUELAS CRUJIENTES

THE CRUNCHY PLUM
Tomatillo, red plum,
and chicharrones

This is an absolute party of a salsa, thanks to crushed chicharrones (beer's best friend). The combination of plums and tomatillos replicates the flavor of prickly pear, assertive and just a little sweet. Then the crunchy chicharrones and pepitas join the festivities and it's like a mariachi band walked into the bar and everyone stood up to dance. The acidic fruit needed that fatty richness to tame its bite. I love piling this texture-crazy salsa on Totopos (page 112) or bigger pieces of chicharrones, naturally.

MAKES 3 CUPS

- 8 medium tomatillos (1 lb/480 g), husked, rinsed, and chopped

- 2 large ripe red or black plums (5.6 oz/160 g), stemmed, seeded, and chopped

- 3 chiles serranos (1.6 oz/45 g), stemmed and thinly sliced

- 2 spring onions or scallions, root end trimmed, thinly sliced (1.6 oz/44 g)

- ¼ cup toasted pepitas/pumpkin seeds (1 oz/30 g)

- 1 cup chopped chicharrones (1 oz/28 g)

- 1 garlic clove, finely grated

- 1½ teaspoons Diamond Crystal kosher salt (0.21 oz/6 g), plus more to taste

SERVING SUGGESTIONS

Plum and pork are made for each other (chops, ribs, pulled pork), or serve with beer, totopos, and more chicharrones as a bar snack.

In a medium bowl, gently stir together the tomatillos, plums, serranos, spring onions, pepitas, chicharrones, garlic, and salt until completely combined. Taste and season with more salt if desired. Let sit, uncovered, for about 15 minutes to allow the plums to soften and the flavors to meld.

Do ahead: The salsa can be made up to 1 day ahead, without the chicharrones and pepitas. Store in an airtight container in the refrigerator and add the chicharrones and pepitas just before serving.

ENSALADA PICANTE

SPICY SLAW
Cabbage, radishes, and habanero

Cabbage is a frequent garnish in Mexico, on everything from tortas to enchiladas, and I want to show it some love. You can use this in the same way as any classic barbecue slaw, as a topping on sandwiches or as a side salad. This recipe is inspired by an unforgettable curtido (tangy slaw) I had in Oaxaca, in which habanero, citrus juice, and red onion infused the cabbage with what I imagined as neon-colored flavors. It only takes 30 minutes for the flavors to meld—though it will mellow and soften over time. Don't we all?

MAKES 6 CUPS

- ¼ medium head green cabbage (14 oz/400 g), cored and thinly sliced
- 6 large radishes (6.5 oz/185 g), trimmed, halved, and thinly sliced
- ¼ medium red onion (3.1 oz/89 g), chopped
- 2 chiles habaneros (0.7 oz/22 g), stemmed, seeded, and chopped
- 1 teaspoon dried oregano, preferably Mexican
- 2 tablespoons fresh lime juice, plus more to taste
- 2 tablespoons fresh orange juice
- 2 teaspoons Diamond Crystal kosher salt (0.28 oz/8 g), plus more to taste

SERVING SUGGESTIONS

With all your summer barbecue favorites, plus pulled pork, brisket tacos, fried chicken, fried fish, and grilled or fried veg.

In a large bowl, toss together the cabbage, radishes, onion, habaneros, oregano, lime juice, orange juice, and salt until completely combined. Let sit, uncovered, for at least 30 minutes to allow the cabbage to soften and the flavors to develop. Taste and season with more salt and lime juice if desired. You can serve immediately or store in the fridge.

Do ahead: The salad can be made up to 3 days ahead. Store in an airtight container in the refrigerator. The flavor will continue to develop as it sits and will taste better the next day.

Vegan carnitas tacos

Chicken tinga tacos

LA REFRESCANTE

REFRESHING
Cucumber, jícama, and orange

Almost as commonly as I've encountered tomatoes in picadas, I've encountered jícama, a crisp tuber with the flavor of a mild pear, consumed all over Mexico. Its texture is as refreshing as a dip in the ocean, and luckily, you can find it easily in the States now. In this salsa, the combination of jícama, cucumber, and orange creates a spa water vibe, while red onion and serrano drop a beat of heat. I especially like this as a summer side salad with barbecue or picnic sandwiches, because the jícama and cucumbers hold up so much better than tomatoes.

MAKES 2 CUPS

- 1 large orange (15 oz/430 g)
- ½ medium jícama (7.5 oz/214 g), peeled and chopped
- ½ medium cucumber (7 oz/198 g), chopped
- ¼ medium red onion (3.1 oz/89 g), chopped
- 3 chiles serranos (1.6 oz/45 g), stemmed and chopped
- 2 tablespoons chopped fresh cilantro leaves with tender stems (0.28 oz/8 g)
- 2 tablespoons fresh lime juice, plus more to taste
- 2 tablespoons fresh orange juice
- 2 teaspoons Diamond Crystal kosher salt (0.28 oz/8 g), plus more to taste

SERVING SUGGESTIONS

Make larger cuts and serve as a side at picnics and barbecues with smoked or grilled meats, pan-fried fish, or grilled veggies; pile onto your next sandwich or wrap in place of tomatoes/pickles.

1. Using a paring knife, remove the peel and white pith from the orange, being careful not to remove too much of the flesh. Slice the citrus into ½-inch-thick rounds, then cut into 1-inch pieces (it looks cool and is less fussy if pieces aren't too exact in shape and size).

2. In a medium bowl, gently stir together the orange, jícama, cucumber, onion, serranos, cilantro, lime juice, orange juice, and salt until completely combined. Taste and season with more salt and lime juice if desired. Let sit, uncovered, for about 10 minutes so the flavors can meld.

Do ahead: The salsa can be made up to 1 day ahead. Store in an airtight container in the refrigerator.

EL MELÓN MÁGICO

THE MAGIC MELON
Cantaloupe, cashews, and ginger

Remember: You can make salsa with whatever you want! It's finding a balance between the ingredients that's key to salsa success. I eat a lot of cantaloupe in Mazatlán, and its mild sweetness is perfect for salsa, as are peaches, nectarines, mangoes, and papaya. Those soft, sweet fruits need crunchy, spicy counterpoints, so I tossed some cashews into the mix, a shake of dried ginger, and chiles pequínes to mimic the dusting of dried chile you'd get with cut fruit on the street in Mexico. It's full of surprises, full of flavor, and full of *life*. Add a handful of salty cheese to transform it into an unexpected salad.

MAKES 2 CUPS

- ¼ large cantaloupe (10.8 oz/306 g), peeled, seeded, and chopped
- ½ medium jícama (7.5 oz/214 g), peeled and chopped
- ¼ medium red onion (3.1 oz/89 g), chopped
- ½ cup salted roasted cashews (2.3 oz/65 g), chopped
- 16 fresh or dried chiles pequínes (0.05 oz/1.5 g), ground or finely chopped
- 1 garlic clove, finely grated
- 1 tablespoon chopped fresh cilantro leaves with tender stems (0.14 oz/4 g)
- ½ teaspoon ground, dried, or freshly grated ginger
- 1 tablespoon fresh lime juice, plus more to taste
- 1½ teaspoons Diamond Crystal kosher salt (0.21 oz/6 g), plus more to taste

SERVING SUGGESTIONS

Add to charcuterie boards; or make it a side salad with cured meats, salty cheeses like ricotta salata, Parmesan, or Cotija; serve alongside a pork sandwich or tacos, Enchiladas, Enfrijoladas, Entomatadas, Enmoladas (see page 234), quesadillas (see page 263), Tostadas (page 113); Thai or Vietnamese dishes with ginger and lemongrass.

In a medium bowl, gently stir together the cantaloupe, jícama, onion, cashews, chiles pequínes, garlic, cilantro, ginger, lime juice, and salt until completely combined. Taste and season with more salt and lime juice if desired. Let sit, uncovered, for about 10 minutes so the flavors can meld.

Do ahead: The salsa can be made up to 1 day ahead. Store in an airtight container in the refrigerator.

Pork
noodle bowl

Grilled veggie
and chicken tacos

AGUACATE AHUMADO

SPICY AVOCADO
Tomato, avocado, and chipotle in adobo

All the salsas in this chapter are fresh, raw, and bright. But this pico de gallo turns a corner. A smoky corner. Finely chopped chipotles in adobo end up glazing the soft pieces of avocado, and it tastes deep and charred, even though it took all of 5 minutes to make. I believe my direct quote after tasting this was "It shouldn't taste this good." But it does.

MAKES 1½ CUPS

- 2   medium Roma tomatoes (8.6 oz/246 g), chopped

- 1   medium avocado (6 oz/170 g), peeled, pitted, and chopped

- ¼   medium white onion (3.1 oz/89 g)

- 5   chipotle chiles in adobo, finely chopped, plus 1 tablespoon adobo sauce

- 1   teaspoon Diamond Crystal kosher salt (0.14 oz/4 g), plus more to taste

SERVING SUGGESTIONS

On a cold-cut sandwich, fried chicken sandwich, Torta Milanesa (page 244), Tostadas de Tinga de Pollo (page 250), onion smash burger, grilled cheese, steak or chicken fajitas, Sonoran-Style Hot Dogs (page 275), or with a bowl of plantain chips.

In a medium bowl, gently stir together the tomatoes, avocado, onion, chipotles, and salt until completely combined. Taste and season with more salt if desired. Let sit, uncovered, for about 10 minutes so the flavors can meld.

Do ahead: The salsa can be made up to 1 day ahead. Store in an airtight container in the refrigerator.

FREEZE THE HEAT
Chipotles out of the can will start to lose their flavor after you've opened them and could go bad after a few weeks in the refrigerator. If you're not planning on using the rest of the can soon, you can transfer them to an airtight container and freeze for later.

BAILE DEL MANGO

DANCE OF THE MANGO
Mango, jícama, and jalapeño

This dish takes inspiration from one of my favorite classic Mexican botanas (snacks)—mango topped with chamoy (a fruity sweet/sour salsa), Tajín (chile/lime seasoning), hot sauce, lime, and salt—but pirouettes into a salsa picante with the addition of red onion, jalapeño, and cilantro. The jícama and cucumber give it a crisp crunch that sets this apart from mango salsas you may have had before. It goes great on any taco, or as a side salad, bringing that sweet, juicy, tropical heat I can never get enough of. You will definitely want to make the OG Mango Botana version, so I've added that recipe here, too.

MAKES 2 CUPS

- 1 large ripe mango Ataúlfo/ Champagne mango (11.2 oz/318 g), peeled, seeded, and chopped

- ¼ large jícama (5.6 oz/158 g), peeled and chopped

- ¼ large cucumber (5.6 oz/160 g), chopped

- ¼ medium red onion (3.1 oz/89 g), chopped

- 2 chiles jalapeños (2.2 oz/62 g), stemmed and chopped

- 2 tablespoons chopped fresh cilantro leaves with tender stems (0.28 oz/8 g)

- 1 tablespoon fresh lime juice, plus more to taste

- 1½ teaspoons Diamond Crystal kosher salt (0.21 oz/6 g), plus more to taste

SERVING SUGGESTIONS

Fish tacos, ceviche, seafood tostadas, grilled meats and veggies, shish kebabs, falafel, shawarma, gyros.

In a medium bowl, gently stir together the mango, jícama, cucumber, onion, jalapeños, cilantro, lime juice, and salt until completely combined. Taste and season with more salt and lime juice if desired. Let sit, uncovered, for about 10 minutes so the flavors can meld.

Mango Botana: Omit the onion, jalapeños, and cilantro. In a medium bowl, gently toss together the mango, jícama, cucumber, lime juice, and a pinch of salt until completely combined. Taste and season with more salt and lime juice if desired. Top with a generous sprinkle of chile en polvo (a ground hot chile like Tajín, not chili powder), a healthy pour of chamoy, and Salsa Picante de Valentina (page 156) or your favorite bottled hot sauce.

Do ahead: The salsa can be made up to 1 day ahead. Store in an airtight container in the refrigerator.

Falafel pita sandwich

RACLETTE

GAME TIME

☀ You've been wondering where it is. Patiently turning by pages of tomato after tomatillo, in search of the dish that makes everyone happy. The salsa that never lasts long, the bowl scraped clean except for a few green streaks. It's time for guacamole. And a little linguistics. Did you know *aguacate* (avocado) comes from the ancient Náhuatl word *ahuacatl* which means testicle? Then the "mole" in guacamole comes from the Náhuatl word *mulli,* which means salsa, *mole* (cooked chile sauce), or *molido* (ground up). Let that be the conversation starter the next time you serve one of these four recipes.

Salt Slowwwly
When adding salt to guacamole, season, stir, and wait 5 minutes to taste. Because of the oil in the avocado, the salt needs more time to dissolve. If you don't wait, you risk oversalting. Learn from my mistakes.

GUACAMOLE A LA RICK

Avocado, onion, and jalapeño

By the book, guacamole is a salsa made with mature avocados smashed and mixed with chile serrano or jalapeño, tomato, onion, and cilantro, and sometimes with a squeeze of lime to prevent oxidation. This comes from the godfather of Mexican cuisine, author of *Diccionario Enciclopédico de la Gastronomía Mexicana,* Ricardo Muñoz Zurita. My version is sans tomatoes because I don't like to risk a mealy, flavorless tomato stealing space in my guacamole. That said, during tomato season, try adding a gorgeous ripe heirloom to your guacamole and you'll understand why Don Ricardo says to do so.

MAKES 3 CUPS

- 3 medium avocados (18.9 oz/538 g), peeled and seeded
- ¼ medium white onion (3.45 oz/98 g), finely chopped
- 2 chiles jalapeños (2.2 oz/66 g), stemmed and finely chopped
- 1 garlic clove, finely grated
- 3 tablespoons chopped fresh cilantro leaves with tender stems (0.42 oz/12 g)
- 2 tablespoons fresh lime juice, plus more to taste
- 1½ teaspoons Diamond Crystal kosher salt (0.21 oz/6 g), plus more to taste

SERVING SUGGESTIONS

You know what to do.

Working in batches, use a molcajete or mortar and pestle (or a medium bowl with a potato masher, large spoon, or forks) to smash the avocados until a chunky paste forms. Transfer to a medium bowl and add the onion, jalapeños, garlic, cilantro, lime juice, and salt and stir to combine. Taste and season with more salt and lime juice if desired.

Do ahead: The guacamole can be made up to 1 day ahead. Press a piece of plastic wrap directly onto the surface of the guacamole to prevent the top from turning brown and store in an airtight container in the refrigerator.

GUACAMOLE CON QUESO FRESCO

Avocado, queso fresco, and pequín

I once had guacamole at a Mexican restaurant on the side of the highway called La Curva outside of Mazatlán. They made their own cheeses and many of their dishes were served with big hunks of queso fresco alongside. I ordered the "special" guacamole, which was about 50/50 queso to avocado. It changed me. The creamy, fresh flavor of the homemade cheese with the rich avocado was decadence on top of more decadence. In my version, I use less cheese so you can still taste the avocado, but follow your heart.

MAKES 2 CUPS

(Double the recipe for 2+ people!)

- 2 medium avocados (14.8 oz/420 g), peeled and seeded
- ¾ cup crumbled queso fresco (4.2 oz/120 g), crema, or farmer cheese
- 16 fresh or dried chiles pequines (0.05 oz/1.5 g), ground or finely chopped
- 1 garlic clove, finely grated
- 1 tablespoon fresh lime juice, plus more to taste
- 1½ teaspoons Diamond Crystal kosher salt (0.21 oz/6 g), plus more to taste

SERVING SUGGESTIONS

Atop rice and beans, chicken enchiladas, or just eat the whole thing with a big bag of Totopos (page 112).

Working in batches, use a molcajete or mortar and pestle (or a medium bowl with a potato masher, large spoon, or forks) to smash the avocados, until a chunky paste forms. Transfer to a medium bowl and add the queso fresco, chiles pequines, garlic, lime juice, and salt and stir to combine. Taste and season with more salt and lime juice if desired.

Do ahead: The guacamole can be made up to 1 day ahead. Press a piece of plastic wrap directly onto the surface of the guacamole to prevent the top from turning brown and store in an airtight container in the refrigerator.

SHOPPING FOR QUESO FRESCO
Queso fresco is mild, milky, and a little crumbly. Try to find one that's made with whole milk for the creamiest flavor. If you have access to farmer cheese where you are, that's a good substitute.

GUACAMOLE CON TOMATILLOS

Blended avocado, tomatillo, and spring onion

While guacamole usually needs to be eaten ASAP, this lighter, blended version stays good in the fridge for days and makes enough to freeze some for later, too. It's an all-purpose salsa to douse on your eggs, fish tacos, pork chops, what have you. And because everything's thrown in the blender, this is a great one to make with harder avocados that wouldn't smash as easily.

MAKES 3½ CUPS

- 2 medium avocados (15.4 oz/438 g), peeled and seeded
- 2 medium tomatillos (4.3 oz/122 g), husked, rinsed, and roughly chopped
- 2 chiles serranos (1.7 oz/50 g), stemmed and roughly chopped
- 1 chile jalapeño (1.9 oz/54 g), stemmed and roughly chopped
- 2 spring onions or scallions, root end trimmed, roughly chopped (1.6 oz/44 g)
- ¼ cup chopped fresh cilantro leaves with tender stems (0.56 oz/16 g)
- 1 garlic clove, peeled but whole
- 4½ teaspoons Diamond Crystal kosher salt (0.63 oz/18 g), plus more to taste

SERVING SUGGESTIONS

Totopos (page 112), chicharrones, quesadillas (see page 263), or almost anything, really.

In a blender, combine the avocados, tomatillos, serranos, jalapeño, spring onions, cilantro, garlic, salt, and ¾ cup water and purée on medium-low speed until smooth. Don't blend above medium speed or your salsa will get airy and have the texture of a smoothie. Taste and season with more salt if desired. For a thinner consistency, add more water, a few tablespoons at a time, and blend.

Do ahead: The guacamole can be made up to 2 days ahead. Press a piece of plastic wrap directly onto the surface of the guacamole to prevent the top from turning brown and store in an airtight container in the refrigerator, or freeze for up to 1 month. (Thaw in the fridge overnight before serving.)

GUACAMOLE DE LA PLAYA

BEACHY GUACAMOLE
Avocado, mango, and
chile de árbol

I could've written an entire book on guacamole based on how many different ones I've had across Mexico. In Guanajuato, I had it with peaches and grapes, and in Zacatecas, tomatoes and crema. I especially love it with escamoles (ant larvae), which are like topping your guacamole with caviar. Insanely good. But start with mango, and work your way up. I made fish tacos one afternoon and served this to a mason repairing my patio who had the grumpy look of an ancient mariner. But when he had this mango-studded guacamole, he lost it. And ate the whole bowl.

MAKES 3 CUPS

- 2 medium avocados (17.2 oz/489 g), peeled and seeded
- 1 large ripe mango Ataúlfo/ Champagne mango (11.2 oz/ 318 g), peeled, seeded, and chopped
- ¼ medium red onion (3.1 oz/89 g), chopped
- 4 fresh or dried chiles de árbol (0.13 oz/3.7 g), stemmed, seeded, and finely ground or chopped
- 1 garlic clove, finely grated
- 1 tablespoon fresh lime juice, plus more to taste
- 1½ teaspoons Diamond Crystal kosher salt (0.21 oz/6 g), plus more to taste

SERVING SUGGESTIONS

The mango wants to be paired with seafood or pork, the avocado wants steak, tortas, but really any meat and any vegetable. You might just eat it from the bowl.

In a medium bowl, gently stir together the avocados, mango, onion, chiles de árbol, garlic, lime juice, and salt until completely combined. Taste and season with salt and lime juice if necessary. Let sit, uncovered, for about 10 minutes so the flavors can meld.

Do ahead: The salsa can be made up to 1 day ahead. Store in an airtight container in the refrigerator.

3-

BLENDED
SALSAS

CHAPTER 3

LICUADAS
—BLENDED SALSAS

✳ I see the $20 Oster three-speed blender everywhere in Mexico, where it's as common as a coffeemaker in the US. It's a permanent fixture on kitchen counters and plugged into extension cords at local taquerias next to the grill so that all the charred salsa veggies can go right from the fire to the blender. I've even heard younger Mexicans refer to them as "molcajetes electricos" (electric molcajetes), which cracks me up. I use either a Vitamix—I'm spoiled—or a Magic Bullet smoothie blender for salsas-for-one. Honestly, I had the Oster once, but I burnt out the motor with a batch of mole, oops. The lesson here is to work with what you got.

A blended salsa is a beautiful thing. It can be satisfyingly smooth or as chunky as one made in a molcajete if you pulse with restraint, and you'll see both textures in this chapter. These recipes show how quickly and easily salsa can be in your life. Let the machine do the work. The truth is, any blender will do (well, maybe not my dad's 1980s Oster Regency Kitchen Center), and you'll have all the salsas in this chapter whirred up to velvety, pourable perfection in under five minutes, minus any prep time.

A Few Blender Tips:

● Always start on low speed for an initial chop, then work your way up to medium-low, but don't go higher or you'll have airy, smoothie-textured salsas . . .

● . . . with the exception of nut- or seed-based salsas, which you should blend on high.

● When you're blending still-hot ingredients, put a kitchen towel over the lid to keep hot stuff from exploding out, and always start on the lowest speed and slowly increase the speed.

● The second your salsa is done and out of the blender, fill the blender jar halfway with water and a drop or two of dish soap, and blend on high to clean and make your life easier down the road.

SERRANO FRITO

FRIED SERRANO
Serrano, lime juice, and parsley

This is inspired by two salsas I had in Oaxaca that were served with a platter of fried corn and cheese empanadas (drool). The two salsas were pretty much the same ingredients, but one was blended raw while the other was made with caramelized vegetables that had been sautéed in oil. The cooked version was sweet, creamy, and spicy, and it easily won my heart. But the raw version was bright, acidic, hot, and deep emerald green. So different, but also so delicious. This recipe is cooked, but if you like, try the raw version by skipping step one in the recipe below, and taste for yourself.

MAKES 1½ CUPS

- 2 tablespoons extra-virgin olive oil
- 6 chiles serranos (3 oz/86 g), stemmed and roughly chopped
- ¼ medium white onion (3.9 oz/112 g), roughly chopped
- 2 garlic cloves, smashed and peeled (but still holding their shape)
- 3 tablespoons chopped fresh parsley leaves with tender stems (0.4 oz/12 g)
- 2 tablespoons fresh lime juice, plus more to taste
- 2 teaspoons Diamond Crystal kosher salt (0.28 oz/8 g), plus more to taste

SERVING SUGGESTIONS

Spoon over tacos; mix with mayonnaise for a spicy green mayo for tortas and wraps; great with grilled meats and vegetables, baked potatoes, crispy smashed potatoes, and steamed veg.

1. In a large skillet, heat the oil over medium-high. Add the serranos, onion, and garlic and cook, tossing occasionally, until the chiles and onion are tender and beginning to brown, 6 to 8 minutes.

2. Transfer the chile mixture, any accumulated juices, and oil to a blender and purée on medium-low speed until the salsa is almost smooth.

3. Transfer to a medium bowl and stir in the parsley, lime juice, and salt. Taste and season with more lime juice and salt if desired.

Do ahead: The salsa can be made up to 5 days ahead. Store in an airtight container in the refrigerator, or freeze for up to 1 month.

OIL IS MAGIC

In salsa, oil can change everything. Its richness tames heat by dulling the capsaicin in the chiles, so you can increase the chiles for more flavor without more heat. It also emulsifies the salsa into a creamy consistency, almost (but not totally) like aioli. If you've ever accidentally made an overly spicy salsa, just stir in olive oil. Learn more about how to tame the heat on page 25.

● Loaded baked potatoes

Iceberg wedge salad

EL CACAHUATE

THE PEANUT
Peanuts, garlic, and chile de árbol

I wanted to capture the flavor of deeply roasted peanut butter in this salsa. The key to concentrating the peanut flavor is to toast the nuts (even if they're already roasted). Then I balance the oil with water to create a pourable consistency without muting the flavor, which can happen if you use too much oil. The salsa's supporting players are caramelized onion, garlic, and toasted chile, creating a nutty-savory sauce you'll want to smother on roasted Brussels sprouts, sweet potatoes, and cauliflower.

MAKES 1½ CUPS

- 1 cup roasted peanuts (4.8 oz/135 g)
- 1 tablespoon vegetable oil
- ¼ medium white onion (3.8 oz/80 g), roughly chopped
- 1 garlic clove, smashed (but still holding its shape)
- 12 fresh or dried chiles de árbol (0.4 oz/12 g), stemmed
- 2 teaspoons Diamond Crystal kosher salt (0.28 oz/8 g), plus more to taste

SERVING SUGGESTIONS

Spoon over tacos, tortas, roasted veggies, shish kebabs, salads, chicken or fish or shellfish. Serve as a dip for raw veggies. Goes well with Lebanese, Persian, Thai, or Vietnamese grilled meats.

1. Heat a large skillet over medium-high. Add the peanuts and toast, tossing frequently, until very fragrant and lightly browned, about 3 minutes. Transfer to a small heatproof bowl and let cool, set aside until ready to use.

2. Add the oil to the same skillet and heat over medium-high. Add the onion and garlic and cook, tossing occasionally, until the onion is tender and beginning to brown, 4 to 6 minutes. Add the chiles de árbol and cook, tossing frequently, until the chiles are fragrant and begin to darken to a brick red color in spots, 1 to 2 minutes.

3. Transfer the chile mixture and any accumulated juices and oil to a blender. Add the peanuts, salt, and 1 cup water and purée on medium speed until almost smooth (there should be very small pieces of peanut, about the size of coarse cornmeal or grits throughout the salsa). It should have the thickness of heavy cream, thin with more water if necessary, and season with more salt if desired.

Do ahead: The salsa can be made up to 5 days ahead. Store in an airtight container in the refrigerator, or freeze for up to 1 month.

SWAP CORNER
Feel free to use almonds, cashews, or macadamias (if you're a millionaire) here, just follow the weight measurement for best results.

SALSA TEJANA

TEXAS SALSA
Roasted peaches, charred habanero, and toasted pecans

This is my favorite salsa in this chapter. I'm a Texas boy, and the flavor of Hill Country peaches and pecans takes me back home. Here, the sweet-smoky charred peaches and toasted pecans create a rich, creamy texture that's woken up with habanero, red onion, and a mixture of lime-orange juice that mimics Yucatecan sour oranges. You might go in with an expectation of what this will taste like, but I swear, you won't see it coming. I devoured it with carnitas tacos with pickled red onions, but it'll add much-needed fat to chicken breasts, bring out the smokiness of grilled meats, and be a good friend to pork chops.

MAKES 2½ CUPS

- 3 large ripe peaches (14 oz/398 g), halved and pitted
- 1 tablespoon vegetable oil, for brushing
- ¼ medium red onion (3.4 oz/96 g), roughly chopped
- 2 garlic cloves, unpeeled
- 1 chile habanero (0.4 oz/12 g), stemmed and halved
- ½ cup raw pecans (1.8 oz/50 g)
- 2 tablespoons fresh lime juice
- 2 tablespoons fresh orange juice
- 2 teaspoons Diamond Crystal kosher salt (0.28 oz/8 g), plus more to taste
- 2 tablespoons chopped fresh basil (0.3 oz/8 g)

SERVING SUGGESTIONS

Spoon over tacos, tortas, carnitas, soups and stews that need a sweet/spicy pick-me-up. Serve as a dip for raw veggies.

1. Line a large cast-iron skillet with a sheet of foil and heat the skillet over high until very hot. Brush the cut sides of the peaches with the oil to prevent sticking. Add the peaches, onion, garlic, and habanero to the pan and cook, using tongs to turn occasionally, until everything is charred on all sides, about 3 minutes for the garlic, 4 minutes for the habanero, and 6 to 8 minutes for the onion and peaches. (Alternatively, arrange an oven rack in the top position and preheat the broiler to high. Arrange the produce on a foil-lined sheet pan and roast under the broiler, turning occasionally, until all sides are charred.) Transfer to a plate to cool. Once cool enough to handle, peel the garlic.

2. Meanwhile, arrange a rack in the center of oven and preheat to 350°F.

3. Arrange the pecans in an even layer on a sheet pan and bake until the pecans are lightly toasted and very fragrant, 9 to 11 minutes. Let cool on the pan until ready to use.

4. Transfer the peaches, onion, garlic, habanero, pecans, lime juice, orange juice, and salt to a blender and purée on medium-low speed until the salsa is almost smooth.

5. Transfer to a medium bowl and stir in the basil. Taste and season with more salt if desired.

Do ahead: The salsa can be made up to 3 days ahead. Store in an airtight container in the refrigerator, or freeze for up to 1 month.

GRILL IT!
If you like to throw peaches on the grill, there's no reason not to take this recipe outside and char your ingredients there instead. Just don't let the habanero fall through the grates.

Pulled BBQ turkey tacos

Ramen bowl

AJONJOLÍ

SESAME
Sesame, tomato, and chiltepín

Sesame is used often in Mexican salsas, but it's rarely showcased front and center. Tahini lovers, this is for you. Toasted sesame and the earthy, sweet-smoky heat of tiny chiltepín chiles are a match made in salsa heaven because the chile doesn't overpower the sesame. The heat is tempered by the sweetness of tomato, garlic, onion, with some acidity from tomatillo. (I don't use actual tahini because the seeds toasted in oil make a bigger flavor without the bitterness I often find in jarred tahini.) The salsa is smooth and gently sandy, and it's just as happy on tacos as it is in ramen or as a dip for gyoza.

MAKES 1¾ CUPS

- 3 tablespoons vegetable oil, divided
- 1 medium Roma tomato (7.4 oz/210 g), roughly chopped
- 1 medium tomatillo (3.5 oz/100 g), roughly chopped
- ¼ medium white onion (3.1 oz/89 g), roughly chopped
- 2 garlic cloves, peeled and smashed (but still holding their shape)
- ⅓ cup raw sesame seeds (1.8 oz/50 g)
- 1 tablespoon fresh or dried chiles chiltepín (0.2 oz/5 g) or 5 chiles de árbol
- 1½ teaspoons Diamond Crystal kosher salt (0.21 oz/6 g), plus more to taste

SERVING SUGGESTIONS

Spoon over tacos, tortas, roasted veggies, egg dishes, fried or scrambled eggs, salads, ramen, pasta, or rice.

1. In a large skillet, heat 2 tablespoons of the oil over medium-high. Add the tomato, tomatillo, onion, and garlic and cook until the onion is tender and beginning to brown and the tomato and tomatillo have broken down, 4 to 6 minutes. Add ¼ cup water to deglaze the skillet, scraping up any browned bits and continue cooking for 30 seconds. Transfer to a medium bowl.

2. Add the remaining 1 tablespoon oil to the same skillet and toast the sesame seeds, tossing frequently, until the seeds begin to toast and pop, about 90 seconds. Add the chiles chiltepín to the skillet and cook, tossing frequently until the chiles are fragrant and begin to darken to a brick red color, about 30 seconds.

3. Transfer the sesame mixture to a blender. Add the salt, tomato mixture, and any accumulated juices and purée on medium speed until almost smooth (there will be small pieces of sesame throughout the salsa and that is okay). It should have the consistency of grits in heavy cream, so thin with more water if necessary and season with more salt if desired.

Do ahead: The salsa can be made up to 5 days ahead. Store in an airtight container in the refrigerator, or freeze for up to 1 month.

EL PEPINO

THE CUCUMBER
Cucumber, tomatillo, and poblano

At the end of the week, I'll blend whatever veg is left in the fridge into a super-fast salsa. This is what happened when I had half of a cucumber, which made an incredibly refreshing yet spicy, tangy, and satisfying salsa verde, with the sweet aroma of cucumber coming through. Feel free to add a handful of about-to-wilt greens (I throw in spinach when I have it). I left them out here because they don't provide much flavor, just a beautiful green color. Another bonus, this salsa stays fresh for days, makes a ton, and freezes well.

MAKES 3 CUPS

- 3 medium tomatillos (7.5 oz/212 g), husked, rinsed, and roughly chopped
- ½ large cucumber (7.5 oz/214 g), roughly chopped
- 2 medium chiles poblanos (9.5 oz/268 g), stemmed, seeded, and roughly chopped
- 3 chiles serranos (1.1 oz/32 g), stemmed and roughly chopped
- ¼ medium white onion (3.7 oz/105 g), roughly chopped
- 1 garlic clove, peeled but whole
- 1 tablespoon Diamond Crystal kosher salt (0.42 oz/12 g), plus more to taste
- 2 tablespoons chopped fresh cilantro leaves and tender stems (0.3 oz/8 g)

SERVING SUGGESTIONS

Spoon over tacos, tortas, or heavier dishes that need a bright counterpoint, like fried fish.

In a blender, combine the tomatillos, cucumber, poblanos, serranos, onion, garlic, and salt and purée on medium-low speed until smooth. Do not be tempted to blend above medium speed or your salsa will get airy and have the texture of a smoothie. Taste and season with more salt if desired. Transfer to a medium bowl and stir in the cilantro.

Do ahead: The salsa can be made up to 3 days ahead. Store in an airtight container in the refrigerator, or freeze for up to 1 month.

Fried tofu

TORTA
MILANESA
PAGE 244

LOS PUERQUITOS

THE LITTLE PIGGIES
Beans, bacon, and chile de árbol

Fritos and cans of bean dip were a fixture of family parties when I was a kid, but I could never get on board with that dip, which had nothing on my dad's bacon-y refried beans. Now that I'm an adult who can do whatever I want, I'm taking things three steps further with this pig-on-pig salsa that combines bacon, lard, and chicharrones, intensifying the pork flavor. I'm not exaggerating when I say I was shoving this down my throat during recipe testing. Not only is it a decadent dip, more pourable than the can, but full-bodied like a fine queso. It also makes the best enfrijoladas ever (see page 234).

MAKES 5 CUPS

- 3 cups low-sodium chicken broth or bean cooking liquid
- 2 teaspoons Diamond Crystal kosher salt (0.28 oz/8 g), plus more to taste
- 1 large chile guajillo (0.4 oz/10 g), stemmed and seeded
- 8 fresh or dried chiles de árbol (0.3 oz/8 g), stemmed
- 2 tablespoons rendered lard (or other animal fats) or vegetable oil
- 4 ounces smoked bacon (113 g), cut crosswise into ½-inch pieces
- ¼ medium white onion (3.7 oz/105 g), roughly chopped
- 1 garlic clove, smashed (but still holding its shape)
- 1 (15-ounce) can black beans, drained and rinsed, or 1½ cups homemade beans, drained
- ½ cup chopped chicharrones (0.5 oz/14 g)

SERVING SUGGESTIONS

With Fritos, of course, as a dip; for enfrijoladas (see page 234); slathered on Torta Milanesa (page 244) and Rick's Breakfast Tacos (page 224); mixed into scrambled eggs.

1. In a medium saucepan, combine the chicken broth, salt, guajillos, and chiles de árbol and bring to a boil over high heat. Cover, reduce to a simmer, and cook for 5 minutes. Remove from the heat and let sit for 10 minutes, until the chiles are very soft and ready to blend. (Why are we boiling the chiles? See page 18.)

2. Meanwhile, in a large skillet, heat the lard over medium-high. Add the bacon and cook, stirring occasionally, until the fat has rendered and the bacon is crispy and deep golden brown, 6 to 8 minutes. Use a slotted spoon to transfer the bacon to a medium bowl, leaving as much fat in the skillet as possible.

3. Add the onion and garlic to the skillet and cook, stirring occasionally, until tender and browned, 5 to 7 minutes. Add the beans and cook, stirring occasionally, until the beans are warmed through, 3 to 5 minutes.

4. Transfer the softened chiles and broth, bacon, and bean mixture to a blender. Add the chicharrones and put on the lid. Cover the top with a kitchen towel and firmly press the lid with your hand to prevent the top from popping off while blending. Purée on medium-low until smooth. It should be the consistency of heavy cream, so thin with water to your liking and season with more salt if desired.

Do ahead: The salsa can be made up to 3 days ahead. Store in an airtight container in the refrigerator, or freeze for up to 1 month.

LA MORITA

LITTLE SMOKED JALAPEÑO
Morita, guajillo, and tomatillo

This is a great summer picnic salsa. I see it as an all-purpose barbecue salsa, with more tang than your typical sauce. The light smokiness of the morita (a lightly smoked and dried small jalapeño, whereas a chipotle is a larger jalapeño that's smoked for a longer time) is begging for some barbecue ribs or brisket—or brisket tacos!—or Quesadillas Las Mejores (page 263). Or all of the above.

MAKES 2 CUPS

- 3   large chiles guajillos (0.7 oz/20 g), stemmed and seeded
- 4   chiles moritas (0.4 oz/10 g), stemmed
- 2   teaspoons Diamond Crystal kosher salt (0.28 oz/8 g), plus more to taste
- 3   medium tomatillos (6.5 oz/185 g), husked and rinsed
- ¼   medium red onion (2.1 oz/60 g)
- 3   garlic cloves, unpeeled

SERVING SUGGESTIONS

All the barbecue and Tostadas de Tinga de Pollo (page 250).

1. In a medium saucepan, combine 1 cup water, the guajillos, moritas, and salt and bring to a boil over high heat. Cover, reduce to a simmer, and cook for 5 minutes. Remove from the heat and let sit for 10 minutes, until the chiles are very soft and ready to blend. (Why are we boiling the chiles? See page 18.)

2. Meanwhile, line a large cast-iron skillet with a sheet of foil and heat the skillet over high until very hot. Add the tomatillos, onion, and garlic and cook, using tongs to turn occasionally, until everything is charred on all sides, about 3 minutes for the garlic, 6 to 8 minutes for the onion, and 8 to 10 minutes for the tomatillos. Transfer to a plate to cool. Once cool enough to handle, peel the garlic.

3. Transfer the softened chiles (and cooking liquid) and the charred vegetables to a blender and purée on high until completely smooth. It should be the consistency of half-and-half, so thin with water if necessary and season with more salt if desired.

Do ahead: The salsa can be made up to 5 days ahead. Store in an airtight container in the refrigerator, or freeze for up to 1 month.

Pulled BBQ
rib sandwich

Elotes (Grilled Mexican Corn)

LA MANTECA

THE LARD
Tomato, tomatillo, and chiltepín

This salsa is a love letter to lard. So much of Mexican cuisine has a grounding back note of lard. You don't taste it outright, but it hums along, giving everything a comforting warmth, an essence of pork. The flavor of lard is meant to be present in this salsa, though, so use the best pork or other animal fat you can find. (Is there duck fat in your freezer? Lucky you.) The flavor reminds me of flour tortillas with bacon and eggs, so I love it on breakfast tacos, but you could also simmer proteins in it for dinner.

MAKES 1½ CUPS

- 3 tablespoons rendered lard, bacon fat, or another animal fat (see Fats, page 14)
- ¼ medium white onion (3.7 oz/105 g), roughly chopped
- 2 garlic cloves, peeled and smashed (but still holding their shape)
- 1 tablespoon fresh or dried chiles chiltepín (0.2 oz/5 g) or 5 chiles de árbol
- 3 medium Roma tomatoes (10.1 oz/288 g), roughly chopped
- 1 medium tomatillo (2.6 oz/75 g), husked, rinsed, and roughly chopped
- 1½ teaspoons Diamond Crystal kosher salt (0.21 oz/6 g), plus more to taste

SERVING SUGGESTIONS

Spoon over breakfast tacos, or dinner tacos for that matter, or simmer meats in the sauce before making tacos.

1. In a large skillet, heat the lard over medium-high. Add the onion and garlic and cook, stirring occasionally, until the onion is tender and just beginning to brown, about 3 minutes. Add the chiles chiltepín and cook, stirring frequently, until the chiles are very fragrant and just beginning to darken to a brick red color, about 15 seconds. Add the tomatoes, tomatillo, and salt and cook, stirring occasionally, until most of the juices have evaporated and they begin to break down, 2 to 3 minutes. Add 2 tablespoons water to deglaze the skillet, scraping up any browned bits and continue cooking for 30 seconds. Let cool slightly.

2. Transfer the tomato mixture and any accumulated juices to a blender and purée on medium-low speed until almost smooth (there will be small pieces of tomato, tomatillo, and chiltepín in the salsa and that is okay). It should be thick but pourable, so thin with more water if necessary and season with more salt if desired.

Do ahead: The salsa can be made up to 5 days ahead. Store in an airtight container in the refrigerator, or freeze for up to 1 month.

LA PASILLA

THE CHILE PASILLA
Pasilla, chile de árbol,
and sour orange

The fact is, sometimes you don't have a pile of tomatillos in the house or canned tomatoes in the cabinet. But I can't have a meal without salsa, and neither should you. This almost instant pantry salsa uses dried chiles (I love the chocolaty notes of pasilla, but use whatever you got), garlic, and some citrus to create a pure chile salsa that reminds me of the hot, bright flavor of unfermented Valentina or Cholula. You won't miss the tomato.

MAKES 1 CUP

- 3 large chiles pasillas (1 oz/30 g), stemmed and seeded
- 5 dried chiles de árbol (0.14 oz/4 g), stemmed
- 1 garlic clove, peeled but whole
- 2 tablespoons extra-virgin olive oil
- 2 tablespoons fresh lime juice
- 2 tablespoons fresh orange juice
- 1½ teaspoons Diamond Crystal kosher salt (0.21 oz/6 g), plus more to taste

SERVING SUGGESTIONS

Spoon over tacos, tortas, soups, or stir it into oil and a splash of vinegar for a salad dressing or any bland dish in need of a savior.

1. In a medium saucepan, combine 1 cup water, the pasillas, and chiles de árbol and bring to a boil. Cover, reduce to a simmer, and cook for 5 minutes. Remove from the heat and let sit for 10 minutes, until the chiles are very soft and ready to blend. (Why are we boiling the chiles? See page 18.)

2. Transfer the chiles, ¼ cup of the cooking liquid, the garlic, olive oil, lime juice, orange juice, and salt to a blender and purée until smooth. It should have the consistency of half-and-half, so thin with more cooking liquid if necessary and season with more salt if desired.

Do ahead: The salsa can be made up to 3 days ahead. Store in an airtight container in the refrigerator, or freeze for up to 1 month.

Sauteed strips of
nopal and onion

Guacamole
toast with
a fried egg

CHILES Y NUEZ DE LA INDIA

CHILES AND CASHEWS
Roasted tomato, cashews, and cascabel

This salsa highlights my love for cashews. They are sweet, nutty, and a little fatty, just like me. And it combines charred tomatoes with smoky morita and spicy cascabeles. If you don't have fresh tomatoes, use canned fire-roasted instead. The tomatoes give a deep caramel flavor that complements the buttery cashews, which you add to the blender at the end of the process for a super-crunchy texture. No one can resist this salsa.

MAKES 2 CUPS

- ⅓ cup cashews (1.8 oz/50 g)
- 6 chiles cascabeles (1.5 oz/42 g), stemmed and seeded
- 2 chiles moritas (0.14 oz/4 g), stemmed
- 4 medium Roma tomatoes (1.7 lb/792 g), cored and left whole
- 2 garlic cloves, peeled but whole
- 2 tablespoons fresh lime juice
- 1½ teaspoons Diamond Crystal kosher salt (0.21 oz/6 g), plus more to taste

SERVING SUGGESTIONS

Serve with sturdy chips, or spoon over tacos, tortas, and everything you can.

1. Arrange a rack in the center of the oven and preheat to 350°F.

2. Arrange the cashews on one side of a sheet pan and the chiles on the other. Toast until the chiles are fragrant, about 5 minutes. Remove the chiles from the pan and continue roasting the nuts, tossing once, until golden brown, 3 to 5 minutes longer. Transfer to a plate to cool.

3. Meanwhile, line a medium cast-iron skillet with a sheet of foil and heat the skillet over high until very hot. Add the tomatoes and cook, using tongs to turn occasionally, until they are charred on all sides, 8 to 10 minutes.

4. Transfer the tomatoes to a blender and add the garlic, lime juice, and salt and purée on medium-low speed until almost smooth. Add the chiles and blend until coarsely chopped. Add the cashews and pulse until coarsely chopped, about 5 pulses. Taste and season with more salt if desired.

Do ahead: The salsa can be made up to 3 days ahead. Store in an airtight container in the refrigerator, or freeze for up to 1 month.

CHIPS & SALSA

You can't have salsa without chips. And while I've bought my fair share of Tostitos in my life, making your own just doesn't compare. The kitchen fills with the scent of toasted corn, then you impatiently grab the hot-out-of-the-oil chip that hisses when it touches cold salsa. I have a few methods here, but my go-to is frying in batches, using a pot of oil that I save and reuse. Making your own chips is also a great way to use up those stale, tasteless corn tortillas in the back of your refrigerator. Miraculously, the hot oil coaxes the corn flavor out of those poor dusty things and gives them a purpose: to transport salsa from the bowl to your mouth with love. And salt.

Fried totopos

TOTOPOS

Tortilla Chips

SERVES 4

Makes enough for 4 portions of Chilaquiles (page 239)

Vegetable oil, for frying

16 tortillas de maíz (stale is best), cut into medium-size wedges

Diamond Crystal kosher salt

1. Line a large heatproof bowl with paper towels. Pour at least 3 inches of oil into a heavy-bottomed medium pot fitted with a deep-fry thermometer. Heat over high until the thermometer registers 350°F.

2. Working in batches if you have a smaller pot (the chips should have some room to float around), fry the tortilla wedges, stirring occasionally, until lightly golden brown and crispy, 3 to 4 minutes. Transfer them to the paper towels and lightly season the totopos with salt.

Do ahead: Totopos can be made 1 day ahead. Store in an airtight container and toast in a 350°F oven or toaster oven until crispy.

OIL-FREE TOTOPOS

Baked Tortilla Chips

SERVES 4

Makes enough for 4 portions of Chilaquiles (page 239)

16 tortillas de maíz (stale is best)

Diamond Crystal kosher salt

1. Arrange racks in the upper and lower thirds of the oven and preheat the oven to 350°F.

2. Arrange the tortillas on two sheet pans (trying not to overlap). Bake the tortillas until they're golden brown in spots and crisp, about 35 to 45 minutes.

3. Let cool slightly and use your hands to break into totopos (chips). Season with salt and serve.

Do ahead: Totopos can be made 1 day ahead. Store in an airtight container and toast in a 350°F oven or toaster oven until crispy

FRIED TOSTADAS

Fried Tortillas

MAKES 12 TOSTADAS

- 1 cup vegetable oil
- 12 tortillas de maíz

  Diamond Crystal kosher salt

1. Line a sheet pan with paper towels and have near the stove. In a small skillet, heat the oil over high until it bubbles immediately when the edge of a tortilla touches the surface.

2. Working with one tortilla at a time, fry the tortilla, turning once, until it's crispy, puffed in places, and deep golden brown, about 1 minute per side.

3. Transfer the tostadas to the paper towels to drain and season with salt while hot. Serve warm.

Do ahead: Tostadas can be made 1 day ahead. Store in an airtight container and toast in a 350°F oven or toaster oven until crispy.

BAKED TOSTADAS

Baked Tortillas

MAKES 6 TOSTADAS

- 6 tortillas de maíz
- 2 tablespoons vegetable oil

  Diamond Crystal kosher salt

1. Arrange a rack in the center of the oven and preheat to 450°F.

2. Brush both sides of the tortillas with the oil. Season with salt and arrange on a sheet pan. Bake the tortillas until they're golden brown in spots and crisp, about 10 minutes. Serve warm.

Do ahead: Tostadas can be made 1 day ahead. Store in an airtight container and toast in a 350°F oven or toaster oven until crispy.

4-

SWEET
HEAT

DULCE

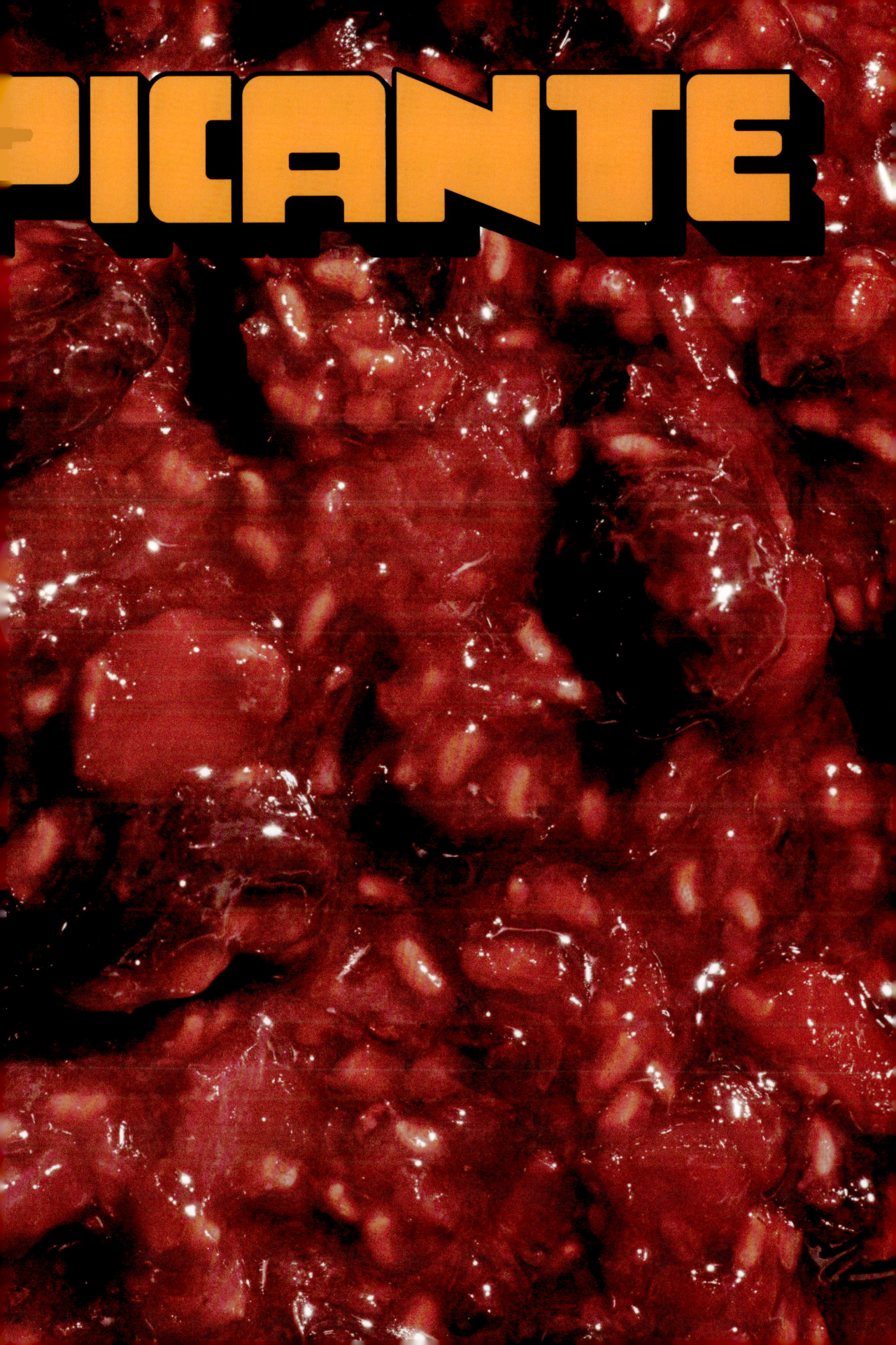

CHAPTER

PICANTE DULCE
—SWEET HEAT

My absolute favorite flavor combination is sweet and spicy. To be clear: This is not a chapter of dessert salsas . . . except for a couple. These are salsas that harness sugar to balance the heat from other ingredients; the sweetness isn't dominant.

In this chapter, we're playing with ingredients that are a little bit different than in the rest of the book. First, there's piloncillo, a typical Mexican sugar with a smoky, caramel flavor (see "I ♥ Piloncillo," right). And while we're not using tomatoes or tomatillos, we still need acid to balance the sweet and tame the spicy. So, there's a lot of vinegar in here, which I often go to when I don't happen to have fresh lime.

In Mexico, I don't encounter that many sweet-leaning salsas. In regions where fruit or sugarcane are grown, those will appear in salsas and mermeladas, which are jammy, though not as thick as the marmalade/jelly you're thinking of. The most memorable sweet salsa I've had here was a habanero jam served with cochinita pibil, that iconic Yucatecan barbecued pork. I fell in love. It had a kiss of sweetness, then a big hit of heat, obviously, and the tang of local citrus. It revealed to me what a huge role sugar has in making the perfect bite of food, whether it's Mexican food or a grilled cheese sandwich. The salsas in this chapter will bring that compulsively edible balance to anything you eat with them.

I ♥ Piloncillo

You're going to see piloncillo throughout this chapter, so go buy some! It's cane sugar that hasn't been super refined, so it contains particles of sugar cane that have minerals, vitamins, and most important: flavor. I pick up caramel, smoky, vegetal notes that molasses-tinged brown sugar doesn't have. Since it comes in solid cones, you'll have to grate it. If it's super hard, try microwaving it for about 20 seconds before grating to soften it up. Then watch as those fluffy bits of dark caramel and toffee fill the inside of your box grater. Heaven.

MERMELADA DE HABANERO CELESTIAL

HEAVENLY HABANERO JAM
Habanero, tequila, and piloncillo

Bright, sunny, spicy, tangy, sweet. Everything that I could ever want in my mouth is in this salsa. Ahem: fruity habaneros, sweet piloncillo, fresh orange juice, and tequila. It's also cooking and chemistry magic. The tequila steals most—but not all—of the heat from the habanero (for more about taming the heat, see page 25), letting its crisp fruity notes come through. (Then the alcohol cooks off.) The salsa has a thick, compote-like consistency with almost translucent, jewel-toned pieces of habanero floating around. I had a version of this with smoky pork tacos, but come on, what couldn't use a little sweet heat?

MAKES 1½ CUPS

- 10 chiles habaneros (4 oz/113 g), stemmed, halved, and seeded
- 2 cups tequila blanco or any clear, 80 proof liquor
- ¼ medium red onion (3.1 oz/89 g), finely chopped
- ½ cup distilled white vinegar
- ⅓ cup fresh orange juice
- 6 tablespoons grated piloncillo (2.8 oz/78 g) or dark brown sugar
- 1½ teaspoons Diamond Crystal kosher salt (0.21 oz/6 g), plus more to taste

SERVING SUGGESTIONS

Carnitas, any Yucatecan food, tender white fish, grilled shrimp, alongside a cheese plate.

1. In a food processor, pulse the habaneros until coarsely chopped. Transfer to a small bowl and stir in the tequila. Let sit uncovered for 1 to 3 hours. The chiles will lose their heat as they soak: After 1 hour, they'll have the heat level of a serrano; after 3 hours, they'll taste like a spicy poblano.

2. Drain the chiles and discard the tequila, or save it to use 1 teaspoon at a time in margaritas (it's killer spicy otherwise).

3. In a medium saucepan, combine 1 cup water, the habaneros, onion, vinegar, orange juice, piloncillo, and salt and bring to a boil over medium-low heat. Cook, stirring occasionally, until the chiles are tender and the liquid is syrupy, 50 minutes to 1 hour. Let cool. Taste and season with more salt if desired.

Do ahead: The salsa can be made up to 1 week ahead. Store in an airtight container in the refrigerator, or freeze for up to 1 month.

SKIP THE TEQUILA, SEEK THE HABANADA
Habanada is a new-ish version of habanero that's been crossbred to be heatless. Crazy, huh? If you're heat averse, look for them in your local grocery store (or grab some seeds); you can use that here and skip the tequila step.

Cochinita pibil tacos

Mushroom and chickpea tacos

MERMELADA DE MOLE GUAJILLO

MOLE-SPICED GUAJILLO JAM
Guajillo, orange juice, and piloncillo

We could all use a little pick-me-up. This salsa does just that. It saves any bland, boring, or meh dish with one spoonful. It has a fragrant, deep flavor that shares some ingredients in common with moles and guisos, those warming spices that make Americans think of holidays, but here, because they all grow together year-round, there's no winter association. This salsa has a beginning, a middle, and an end: sweet chile to start; sharp bite of onion; and the lingering spice of peppercorn, oregano, and clove. It pairs especially well with vegetables like roasted cauliflower steaks, where it can sink into the floret's crevices and make every bite delectably *sabroso*.

MAKES 1 CUP

- 10 large chiles guajillos (3.9 oz/112 g), stemmed and seeded
- 2 chiles cascabeles (0.7 oz/22 g) or 1 dried chiles de árbol, stemmed and seeded
- ½ medium white onion (7.2 oz/205 g), finely chopped
- 2 garlic cloves, peeled but whole
- ½ cup apple cider vinegar
- ⅓ cup fresh orange juice
- 6 tablespoons grated piloncillo (2.8 oz/78 g) or dark brown sugar
- 1½ teaspoons Diamond Crystal kosher salt (0.21 oz/6 g), plus more to taste
- 1 teaspoon black peppercorns
- 1 teaspoon dried oregano, preferably Mexican
- 2 whole cloves
- 1 wide strip orange zest

SERVING SUGGESTIONS

Vegetarian tacos, skinless boneless (boring) chicken breasts, stirred into white rice or stews.

1. In a blender, combine the guajillos, cascabeles, onion, garlic, vinegar, orange juice, piloncillo, salt, peppercorns, oregano, and cloves and purée on high speed until a coarsely ground sauce forms, similar to the consistency of a marinara (there might be pea-size pieces of chile and that's okay).

2. In a medium saucepan, combine the chile purée and 1 cup water and bring to a low simmer over medium-low heat. Cook, stirring occasionally, until the chiles pieces are tender and any liquid is thick and syrupy, 50 minutes to 1 hour.

3. Add the orange zest and let cool (the orange flavor will permeate as it sits). Taste and season with more salt if desired.

Do ahead: The salsa can be made up to 1 week ahead. Store in an airtight container in the refrigerator, or freeze for up to 1 month.

CHOCOLATE PICANTE

Chocolate, piloncillo, and chile de árbol

It has to be said: This is your spicy Hershey's syrup. I started with the almost cliché American concept of "Mexican chocolate" (in which there's always a pinch of cayenne) and then I worked in some of the technique of making dulce de leche for a thick, pourable—or dunkable, which is how I like to use it with conchas—salsa that's creamy and sweet with the slightest hint of heat. I would use this mostly as a dessert salsa or hot fudge sauce.

MAKES 2½ CUPS

- ¼ cup grated piloncillo (2 oz/54 g) or dark brown sugar
- 2 tablespoons agave syrup or honey
- ¼ teaspoon Diamond Crystal kosher salt (0.03 oz/1 g)
- ¾ cup heavy cream
- ¼ cup whole milk
- 2 tablespoons unsalted butter
- 8 ounces (226 g) bittersweet chocolate (60% to 72% cacao), chopped
- ½ teaspoon ground canela or cinnamon
- 1 teaspoon ground chile de árbol or cayenne pepper

SERVING SUGGESTIONS

Drizzle over ice cream, cakes, waffles, pancakes, sundaes, conchas, and of course, churros (page 137).

1. In a heavy-bottomed medium saucepan, bring the piloncillo, agave syrup, salt, and 2 tablespoons water to a boil over medium-high heat, swirling to dissolve the sugar. Boil, without stirring, until an instant-read thermometer registers 265°F, 8 to 10 minutes. Add the cream, milk, and butter and whisk until the butter is melted and the mixture is smooth.

2. Remove from the heat and add the chocolate, canela, and chile de árbol and whisk until melted and the mixture is smooth. Transfer to a heatproof medium bowl and serve warm.

Do ahead: The salsa can be made up to 1 week ahead. Store in an airtight container in the refrigerator. Before serving, reheat in the microwave in 10-second intervals, stirring occasionally, until heated through.

CANELA, MEXICAN CINNAMON
Cassia cinnamon—the type commonly used in the US—is spicy like a box of Red Hots candy, whereas canela, aka Ceylon cinnamon, has a softer, more floral flavor. Each has its purpose! But in this recipe, canela's gentle warmth pairs with the spice of the chile for a subtle, not overpowering heat.

Concha ice cream sandwich

• Ricotta toast

MERMELADA PICANTE DE BAYA DE VERANO

SPICY SUMMER BERRY JAM
Berries, ginger, and chile de árbol

Remember that grilled cheese I mentioned? This is its moment. Because you haven't lived until you've slathered a layer of this spicy berry jam on an oozy grilled cheese. This is the perfect summer berry salsa, so if your berries are super sweet, cut the sugar back by a few tablespoons. I ate my batch with savory foods, but if you want to use this on a dessert (atop a pound cake or ice cream), increase the sugar to ½ cup.

MAKES 1 CUP

- 1 pound mixed fresh berries (453 g), such as raspberries, blackberries, blueberries, and/or chopped strawberries
- ⅓ cup granulated sugar (2.3 oz/66 g)
- 2 tablespoons chopped candied ginger
- 1 teaspoon ground chile de árbol or cayenne pepper

  Diamond Crystal kosher salt

SERVING SUGGESTIONS

Grilled cheese or quesadillas (see page 263), turkey sandwiches, breakfast breads and pastries, grilled chicken, pork chops, or cheese plates.

In a medium saucepan, combine the berries, sugar, ginger, chile de árbol, and a pinch of salt and stir together, until the berries are coated. Set over medium heat and cook, stirring occasionally and skimming the foam off the top, until the berries are very tender and the sauce is slightly thick and jammy, about 10 minutes. Remove from the heat and set aside until ready to serve.

Do ahead: The salsa can be made up to 5 days ahead. Store in an airtight container in the refrigerator, or freeze for up to 1 month.

CARAMELO DE TEQUILA CON SAL

SALTED TEQUILA CARAMEL
Sugar, cream, and tequila

This is a classic caramel with a roasted agave flavor from the reposado tequila (which is often aged in old bourbon barrels, imparting even more caramel notes). This is not exactly a tequila-flavored caramel. Instead, the tequila acts sort of like a vanilla bean; it's not overpowering—it just makes it more caramelly and more delicious. Drizzle this over ice cream, conchas, brownies, and birthday cakes. Or dip strawberries in it and be happy.

MAKES 1 CUP

- 1 cup granulated sugar (7 oz/200 g)
- ½ cup heavy cream
- 6 tablespoons unsalted butter (3 oz/85 g), cut into 6 pieces
- 1 teaspoon Diamond Crystal kosher salt (0.14 oz/4 g)
- ¼ cup tequila reposado

SERVING SUGGESTIONS

You know what to do. Ice cream, brownies, crepes, plates of apples.

1. In a medium saucepan, bring the sugar and ¼ cup water to a boil in a small saucepan over medium-high heat, swirling the pan occasionally without stirring. Cook until the caramel is deep amber (about 365°F on a candy thermometer), about 10 minutes.

2. Remove the pan from the heat and add the cream, butter, and salt (the mixture will bubble vigorously). When the mixture has stopped bubbling, still off heat, add the tequila. Return it to medium-high heat and cook, swirling the pan occasionally, until the caramel comes back to the boil and you can no longer smell raw alcohol. Boil for 1 minute (until it reaches about 220°F again on a candy thermometer). Remove the pan from heat and let cool. The caramel will thicken as it sits.

Do ahead: The salsa can be made up to 1 month ahead. Store in an airtight container in the refrigerator. Before serving, reheat in the microwave in 10-second intervals, stirring occasionally, until heated through.

SWAP CORNER
Swap the tequila for bourbon or rye whiskey for a deeper caramel and boozy flavor, if you're into that kind of thing.

Bananas foster

Spatchcock
grilled chicken

SALSA "BBQ" DE ALBARICOQUE Y CHIPOTLE

APRICOT-CHIPOTLE BARBECUE SAUCE
Apricots, chipotle, and rice vinegar

Whenever I have pints of leftover salsa lying around, which happened a lot during the making of this book, I dump them on chicken as a marinade for grilling or roasting. This one, with dried apricots, reminded me of my favorite barbecue sauces in Texas, which always seem to begin with a store-bought sauce and then get doctored up into something entirely new, and sometimes, a li'l sweet. I also love that all the ingredients in this recipe are pantry staples, so I usually don't have to shop for it. The smoky chipotle counters the sugar and complements any food with burnt ends or char marks. Ribs? Genius.

MAKES 3 CUPS

- 1 cup dried apricots (5.8 oz/165 g)
- 5 chipotle chiles in adobo plus 2 tablespoons adobo sauce (or 5 chiles moritas)
- 1 garlic clove, peeled but whole
- 1 fresh thyme sprig or ½ teaspoon dried thyme
- 2 whole cloves
- 2 teaspoons Diamond Crystal kosher salt (0.28 oz/8 g), plus more to taste
- 2 tablespoons seasoned rice vinegar or white wine vinegar

SERVING SUGGESTIONS

Barbecue of all kinds, but especially grilled chicken, brisket, ribs, and charred vegetables; Tostadas de Tinga de Pollo (page 250).

1. In a medium saucepan, combine 2½ cups water, the apricots, chipotles, adobo sauce, garlic, thyme, cloves, and salt and bring to a boil. Cover, reduce to a simmer, and cook for 5 minutes. Remove from the heat, and let sit for 10 minutes, until the apricots are plump, very soft, and ready to blend.

2. Transfer the apricot mixture, cooking liquid, and vinegar to a blender and purée until smooth. It should be the consistency of pourable yogurt, so thin with water if necessary and season with more salt if desired.

Do ahead: The salsa can be made up to 1 week ahead. Store in an airtight container in the refrigerator, or freeze for up to 1 month.

SWAP CORNER
Instead of dried apricots, you could use dried apples, pears, peaches, or plump golden raisins instead, or even dried mango, which would make a fun tropical variation.

SABE A MERMELADA DE TOCINO

TASTES-LIKE-BACON JAM
Morita, piloncillo, and cider vinegar

Only there's no bacon in it. Chiles moritas are lightly smoked and have a natural sweetness that I wanted to play with in this salsa, but I never expected the result: a complex, savory salsa that reminds me of bacon jam. It's the hard-cooked, caramelized onion that does it (and that's a trick I use for vegan refried beans, too), creating that bitterness you get from the crispy burnt edges of bacon. But also, the piloncillo, which brings a molasses-like sweetness. I'd recommend spooning this thick, sweet-savory sauce anywhere you'd want bacon, from breakfast tacos to sandwiches to loaded baked potatoes.

MAKES 1¼ CUPS

- 5 chiles moritas (0.5 oz/15 g), stemmed
- 2 tablespoons extra-virgin olive oil
- ½ medium white onion (7.4 oz/210 g), sliced
- 4 garlic cloves, peeled and smashed (but still holding their shape)
- 1½ teaspoons Diamond Crystal kosher salt (0.2 oz/6 g), plus more to taste
- ½ teaspoon dried oregano, preferably Mexican
- 2 dried bay leaves
- 2 teaspoons grated piloncillo (0.14 oz/8 g) or dark brown sugar, plus more to taste
- 1 tablespoon apple cider vinegar

SERVING SUGGESTIONS

Use as a flavor enhancer in vegan dishes, especially soups and stews, or mix with mayo as a sandwich condiment (you're welcome).

1. In a small saucepan, bring 1 cup water and the moritas to a boil over high heat. Cover, reduce to a simmer, and cook for 5 minutes. Remove from the heat and let sit for 10 minutes, until the moritas are plump and very soft. Drain and set the chiles aside until ready to blend. (Why are we boiling the chiles? See page 18.)

2. In a medium skillet, heat the oil over medium-high. Add the onion, garlic, and salt and cook, tossing occasionally, until the onion is deep golden brown around the edges, 6 to 8 minutes. Add the oregano, bay leaves, piloncillo, and 1 cup water and bring to a boil. Remove from the heat and transfer to a blender.

3. Add the reserved moritas and vinegar to the blender and purée on medium-low speed until the salsa is almost smooth. Transfer to a medium bowl and taste and season with more salt and piloncillo if desired.

Do ahead: The salsa can be made up to 5 days ahead. Store in an airtight container in the refrigerator, or freeze for up to 1 month.

Roasted whole cauliflower

Tomato and tomatillo panzanella

SALSA DE JAMAICA

HIBISCUS SALSA
Hibiscus flowers, red onion,
and chile de árbol

This recipe is a two-for-one: salsa and agua fresca. Flor de jamaica (hibiscus flowers) are used not just to make the refreshing drink, but the boiled flowers are also used in guisos (stews/braises) and taco fillings. I've never seen them in a salsa de mesa (table salsa), so I thought: Why not? You can use the jamaica cooking liquid to make an agua fresca. For the salsa, the cooked flowers are combined with just enough sugar to balance the pucker, plus onion, garlic, and chile. This salsa has a cranberry sauce–like versatility for all those big holiday roasts, or as a chutney-like salsa that pairs well with Indian food.

MAKES 2 CUPS

- 2 cups dried hibiscus flowers (1.8 oz/50 g)
- ¼ cup extra-virgin olive oil
- ½ medium red onion (7.5 oz/212 g), sliced
- 3 garlic cloves, sliced
- 2 teaspoons Diamond Crystal kosher salt (0.28 oz/8 g), plus more to taste
- 7 fresh or dried chiles de árbol (0.25 oz/7 g), stemmed
- 3 tablespoons granulated sugar (1.3 oz/36 g), plus more to taste
- ½ teaspoon ground allspice or pumpkin pie spice

SERVING SUGGESTIONS

Serve warm with holiday roast beef, turkey, as a glaze for ham, or serve cold with pork shoulder tacos, grilled Halloumi, baked Brie, turkey sandwiches.

1. Add the hibiscus to a medium saucepan, fill it with water, and stir vigorously. Drain in a colander, discard the water, and return the hibiscus to the pot. Add 4 cups fresh water to the pot and bring to a boil over high heat. Cover, reduce to a simmer, and cook for 10 minutes. Set a sieve over a bowl and drain the flowers, reserving the cooking liquid. Set both aside separately until ready to use.

2. In a medium skillet, heat the oil over medium-high. Add the onion, garlic, and salt and cook, tossing occasionally, until the onion is deep golden brown around the edges, 6 to 8 minutes.

3. Add the chiles de árbol and cook, tossing frequently, until very fragrant and bright brick red, about 1 minute. Add the sugar, allspice, 1 cup water, reserved hibiscus flowers, and ½ cup of the reserved hibiscus cooking liquid and bring to a boil. Remove from the heat.

4. Transfer the mixture to a blender and purée on medium-low speed until the salsa is almost smooth. Transfer to a medium bowl and taste and season with more salt and sugar if desired. Thin with additional cooking liquid if necessary.

Do ahead: The salsa can be made up to 5 days ahead. Store in an airtight container in the refrigerator, or freeze for up to 1 month.

AGUA FRESCA DE JAMAICA
To make a glass of agua fresca de jamaica, fill a tall glass with ice and pour over about ½ cup of the jamaica cooking liquid. (It's basically a concentrate.) Top with cold water (or sparkling, if you're feeling bubbly) and stir in sugar or simple syrup to taste. Add more or less water depending on how tart you like it. The jamaica concentrate will last in the refrigerator for 5 days.

ICONIC SOS

✳️ There are sweet sauces I had to include in this chapter, but I couldn't separate them from their complete dish. It would just be cruel. The first is Chiles en Nogada (page 140), a saucy and stuffed chile dish that celebrates Mexican Independence, and the other is churros (see page 137), a dish that celebrates, well, churros.

SALSA DE CHOCOLATE Y VAINILLA

Vanilla Chocolate Sauce

This is not just any chocolate salsa. When I made it (with churros) for a dinner at the James Beard House in New York, the diners licked their bowls clean as if this dessert were about the sauce, not the churros (which were perfect, mind you). The use of an expensive vanilla bean—I know!—is glorious. Half is for the sauce, the other half is for the churro batter. The vanilla bean rounds out the chocolate and makes the flavor ethereal, and I start to float outside my body. I'm sorry, vanilla extract is going to be *good*, but not the same. Either way, though, the texture of this sauce is pudding-like and melts in your mouth.

MAKES 1½ CUPS

- ½ vanilla bean, split lengthwise, or 2 teaspoons pure vanilla extract
- 1 cup heavy cream
- 5 tablespoons grated piloncillo (2.3 oz/65 g), or dark brown sugar
- 1 tablespoon unsweetened cocoa powder
- ⅛ teaspoon Diamond Crystal kosher salt
- 3 ounces (85 g) bittersweet chocolate (60% to 72% cacao), chopped

1. Scrape the vanilla seeds into a small saucepan. Save the pod for another use. (At least, stick it in a jar with sugar, and there: You have vanilla sugar.)

2. Add the cream, piloncillo, cocoa powder, and salt and cook over medium-high heat, whisking occasionally, until the sugar is dissolved, no lumps of cocoa powder remain, and the mixture is simmering, about 4 minutes.

3. Remove from the heat and add the chocolate, stirring to melt. Keep warm over very low heat until ready to serve.

Do ahead: The salsa can be made up to 1 day ahead. Store the salsa in an airtight container in the refrigerator and rewarm before serving.

CHURROS CON SALSA DE CHOCOLATE Y VAINILLA

Fried choux pastry with vanilla chocolate sauce

These churros are just a vehicle for the Salsa de Chocolate y Vainilla (page 136), but it would be a crime not to include them, too. By themselves, they're crisp and airy, tossed with a canela sugar that makes them incredibly delicious even when sauceless. But you know how I feel about the sauce.

MAKES ABOUT 26 CHURROS

- 1 tablespoon ground canela (see page 122) or cinnamon
- 1 cup plus 1 tablespoon granulated sugar (7.5 oz/212 g)
- ½ vanilla bean, split lengthwise, or 2 teaspoons pure vanilla extract
- ½ cup whole milk
- 6 tablespoons unsalted butter (3 oz/85 g)
- 1 teaspoon Diamond Crystal kosher salt (0.14 oz/4 g)
- 1 cup all-purpose flour (4.4 oz/125 g)
- 3 large eggs

  Vegetable oil (about 3 quarts), for deep-frying

  Salsa de Chocolate y Vainilla (page 136), warmed, for serving

SPECIAL EQUIPMENT

Pastry bag and a large closed star tip

Do ahead: The dough can be made up to 1 day ahead. Store the dough in the refrigerator in a pastry bag with all the air squeezed out. Bring to room temperature before frying.

1. In a large bowl, whisk together the canela and 1 cup of the sugar until completely combined. Set aside.

2. In a medium saucepan, combine the vanilla bean, ½ cup water, the milk, butter, salt, and the remaining 1 tablespoon sugar and bring to a simmer over medium-high heat. Using a wooden spoon, add the flour and vigorously stir until the dough comes together, about 30 seconds. Transfer to a stand mixer or a large bowl; remove the vanilla pod. Let cool for 5 minutes.

3. Fit a pastry bag with a large closed star tip. Attach the paddle onto the stand mixer and start beating the dough on medium-low speed (or stir vigorously with a wooden spoon). Add the eggs, one at a time, making sure to incorporate each egg before adding the next. The dough will look broken at first; continue to beat, scraping the bowl occasionally, until the dough comes back together and is smooth, glossy, and stretches without retracting or breaking when pulled. Spoon the dough into the prepared pastry bag.

4. Line a baking sheet with paper towels and set near the stove. Pour oil into a large heavy-bottomed pot so that it comes halfway up the sides. Fit the pot with a deep-fry thermometer and heat over high until the thermometer registers 350°F.

5. Holding the bag at an angle so the tip is a few inches above the surface of oil, squeeze out the dough, moving the bag as you squeeze so the dough is piped in a 6-inch length into the oil. Using a paring knife, cut off the dough at the tip to release it into the oil. Repeat the process to make 4 more dough lengths. Fry the churros, turning once and adjusting the heat as needed to maintain the oil temperature, until golden brown on all sides, 2 to 3 minutes per side. Transfer the churros to the paper towels to drain. Repeat with the remaining dough.

6. Toss the warm churros in the canela/sugar mixture. Serve with warm salsa de chocolate.

SALSA NOGADA

WALNUT SAUCE
Walnuts and cream

This is a salsa unlike any other I'd had before. It's not spicy, but a simple mix of cream, a touch of sugar, and walnuts. (Mine isn't crazy sweet, but I've had some versions that taste like melted ice cream.) It's one half of the national dish of Mexico, Chiles en Nogada (page 140), where the heat from the poblanos is cooled off with this sauce—though if you want to just make the walnut salsa and drizzle it over a bowl of fruit or slice of pie, I won't tell.

MAKES 2 CUPS

- 2¼ cups raw walnuts (4.4 oz/125 g)
- ¾ cup crema, crème fraîche, or sour cream
- ¾ cup heavy cream
- 1 tablespoon granulated sugar
- 1½ teaspoons Diamond Crystal kosher salt (0.21 oz/6 g), plus more to taste

SERVING SUGGESTIONS

Ice cream, fresh or roasted fruit, turkey, sweet potatoes, roasted plantains.

In a blender, combine 1 cup water, the walnuts, crema, heavy cream, sugar, and salt and purée until completely smooth and the consistency of heavy cream. Season with more salt and thin with more water if necessary.

Do ahead: The salsa can be made up to 2 days ahead. Store in an airtight container in the refrigerator, or freeze for up to 1 month.

CHILES EN NOGADA

CHILES IN WALNUT SAUCE
Stuffed, roasted poblanos in a creamy walnut sauce

This iconic dish that re-creates the colors of the Mexican flag (green, white, and red), was invented by nuns in Puebla in 1821. It's eaten every year for Mexican Independence (September 16) and throughout September, but that never feels like enough for me. The sweet-tart pomegranate seeds burst in your mouth while the salsa nogada coats your palate with a nutty, creamy, slightly funky flavor that is a counterpoint to the roasted chile and the sweet-savory picadillo inside.

SERVES 8

PICADILLO

- 5 medium Roma tomatoes (16.9 oz/480 g), stemmed and cored
- 2 tablespoons rendered lard
- 1 pound (453 g) ground pork, preferably not lean
- ½ medium white onion (7.4 oz/210 g), chopped
- ½ firm-ripe plantain (5.9 oz/168 g), peeled and chopped
- ½ sweet-tart apple (3.2 oz/91 g), such as Winesap or Pink Lady, peeled, cored, and chopped
- ½ firm sweet pear (3.1 oz/89 g), such as Bosc or Anjou, peeled, cored, and chopped
- 4 garlic cloves, finely grated
- 2 tablespoons Diamond Crystal kosher salt (0.84 oz/24 g), plus more to taste
- 1 teaspoon dried Mexican oregano
- 1 teaspoon freshly ground black pepper, plus more to taste
- ½ teaspoon ground cinnamon
- ¼ teaspoon ground cloves
- ¼ cup dry sherry

- ½ large ripe peach (2.3 oz/66 g), pitted and chopped
- ¼ cup raw almonds, chopped
- ⅓ cup golden raisins
- ⅓ cup pitted Spanish green olives
- ½ teaspoon finely grated lemon zest
- 2 tablespoons chopped fresh parsley leaves and tender stems (0.3 oz/8 g)
- 1 tablespoon fresh lemon juice

ASSEMBLY

- 8 large chiles poblanos (2.6 lb/1.2 kg)
- Salsa Nogada (page 138), for serving
- 1 cup pomegranate seeds, for garnish
- ½ cup parsley leaves and tender stems (1 oz/30 g), for garnish

1. MAKE THE PICADILLO: Line a large cast-iron skillet with a sheet of foil and heat the skillet over high until very hot. Add the tomatoes and cook, using tongs to turn occasionally, until they are charred on all sides, 8 to 10 minutes. (Alternatively, arrange an oven rack in the top position and preheat the broiler to high. Arrange the tomatoes on a foil-lined sheet pan and roast under the broiler, turning occasionally, until all sides are charred.) Transfer to a heatproof bowl and let sit. When cool enough to handle, crush with your hands, a potato masher, or fork until no large pieces remain. Set aside until ready to use.

2. Remove and discard the foil from the skillet

and heat the lard over high. Spread the pork in an even layer and cook undisturbed until lightly browned, about 3 minutes. Toss and continue to cook, breaking up any clumps with the back of a spoon and scraping up any browned bits from the bottom, until the meat is lightly browned on both sides, 4 to 6 minutes. Using a slotted spoon, transfer the browned meat to a large bowl and set aside.

3. Reduce the heat under the skillet to medium and cook the onion, plantain, apple, pear, garlic, and salt, stirring occasionally, until tender but not browned, 10 to 12 minutes. Add the oregano, black pepper, cinnamon, and clove and cook, stirring frequently, until very fragrant, about 1 minute. Add the sherry and cook, stirring occasionally, until most of the liquid has evaporated and no longer smells of alcohol, about 2 minutes.

4. Stir in the peach, almonds, raisins, and reserved tomatoes and cook, stirring occasionally, until most of the liquid has evaporated, 5 to 7 minutes. Add the cooked pork, olives, lemon zest, and 1 cup water and cook, stirring occasionally, until all the liquid has evaporated, the vegetables and fruit are tender, and the pork is cooked through, 10 to 15 minutes.

5. Stir in the parsley and lemon juice, season with more salt and pepper, if desired, and let sit until ready to use.

6. MEANWHILE, TO ASSEMBLE: Roast the chiles either on the stovetop, under the broiler, or on an outdoor grill. When roasted, the chiles should still be firm, bright green, and hold their shape.

To roast the chiles on a gas stove: Turn all of the burners to high and set 2 poblanos on each grate. Char, using tongs to turn them occasionally, until all sides are charred, about 4 minutes per side.

To roast the chiles under the broiler: Arrange a rack in the top position and preheat the broiler to high. Set the poblanos on a sheet pan and position under the broiler, turning occasionally, until all sides are charred, 2 to 3 minutes per side.

To roast the chiles on a grill: Prepare a charcoal or gas grill for high heat. Set the poblanos directly on the grate and grill, using tongs to turn them as they char on all sides, about 4 minutes per side.

7. Transfer the chiles to a large bowl, cover the bowl tightly with plastic wrap (or the leftover foil you used for the tomatoes), and let the chiles steam for 5 minutes. When cool enough to handle, peel the skin from the chiles, leaving the stem intact.

8. Using a small sharp knife, make a 2-inch cut (about 1 inch from the top) lengthwise down the side of each poblano and carefully remove the seeds and ribs.

9. Place the poblanos cut-side up on a sheet pan and fill each with ½ cup of the picadillo, gently pressing the filling into the chiles with the back of a spoon, being careful not to overstuff and split the sides. Set aside until ready to serve.

10. Serve the stuffed chiles at room temperature, covered in Salsa Nogada, pomegranate seeds, and parsley leaves.

Do ahead: The picadillo can be made up to 2 days ahead. Store in an airtight container in the refrigerator, or freeze for up to 1 month.

5 - ENCU

**PICKLES
& HOT SAUCES**

Y PICAN

ENCURTIDOS Y PICANTES
—PICKLES & HOT SAUCES

☀️ Before you skip ahead thinking fermented hot sauces and pickles are intimidating to make—wait a sec. It's not that big of a deal. The truth is, I often make a salsa and then just . . . leave it on my counter for 3 or 4 days. The flavor deepens and evolves, getting exponentially better. On day one, the ingredients seem big and bold, each fighting for their solo moment. By day three, harmony sets in as the chile's heat mellows and the spices soak into the onions and other ingredients. Then that fermented tang pulls everything together and I'm in love.

To be clear, most of these recipes are not for canning to stockpile in your basement. They are quick, 2- to 4-day ferments and semiquick-pickled vegetables. The recipes are written with the flexibility to make them your own, using the spices and vegetables you prefer. (Experiment! Have fun!)

A few recipes do take around a month, depending on where you live (colder kitchen? Longer ferment time). For those, you'll need a scale, attention to food safety (I'll help you there), and patience—but there's a huge payoff, because a fermented hot sauce can last so much longer in the fridge, ready to be doused on anything. Once you've made your own, it's hard to go back to store-bought, but I'd be lying if I told you there wasn't a giant bottle of Valentina in my cupboard right now. I love that stuff so much I wrote a recipe that replicates it on page 156. I'll let you tell me which you think is better.

Tips for Fermenting

● Use clean mason jars (dishwasher-clean is great).

● When you taste the sauce every day, use a fresh spoon . . .

● . . . and don't double-dip!

● Wear disposable gloves if you stick your hands in the jar to rearrange the weights.

● If it smells vaguely of beer, it's probably time to put it in the fridge.

● If it smells bad, it's bad.

Are We There Yet?

Use a clean spoon to taste the pickles/brine every day to note how the flavors have changed. Maybe you're happy with it on day one, when the pickles are bright, loud, and clear. Cool. Put it in the fridge. I keep tasting until I notice that the flavor *hasn't* changed. For the quick ferments at the start of this chapter, it's been the 3-day mark for me lately, but if your kitchen is colder, it might take 4 or 5.

VERDURAS ENCURTIDAS

PICKLED VEGETABLES
Red onion, jalapeño, and carrot

Here are your all-purpose Mexican pickled veg. We've got a little bit of everything, so when you need pickled onions on a taco, they're there. When you want pickled jalapeños on a sandwich, they're there. When you crave pickled carrots with your rice bowl, they're there. Spoon some of the brine into mayo. Chop a handful of the veg up to season a quick slaw. See what I mean? Freedom. As the vegetables pickle in the brine, looking pretty on your counter, the carrot will soak up the warmth of the spices in the mix, the jalapeño will mellow, and everything will take on that perfect sweet, salty, tangy pickled flavor.

MAKES 1 QUART/LITER

- 1 medium red onion (12.5 oz/356 g), thinly sliced
- 4 chiles jalapeños (4.4 oz/124 g), rinsed, stemmed, and chopped
- 2 medium carrots (7.8 oz/221 g), washed and cut into matchsticks
- 1 tablespoon black peppercorns
- 1 tablespoon allspice berries
- 2 cups distilled white vinegar
- ⅓ cup granulated sugar
- 4½ teaspoons Diamond Crystal kosher salt (0.6 oz/18 g)
- 1 dried bay leaf
- 1 tablespoon dried oregano, preferably Mexican
- 1 orange, well rinsed, zest removed in wide strips
- 2 tablespoons fresh orange juice
- 2 tablespoons fresh lime juice
- 2 garlic cloves, peeled and smashed (but still holding their shape)

SPECIAL EQUIPMENT

1-quart/liter nonreactive container with a lid. Glass, ceramic, stainless steel, food-grade plastic, and silicone will all work.

1. In a 1-quart/liter nonreactive container with a lid, pack the onion, jalapeños, and carrots.

2. In a large dry saucepan, toast the peppercorns and allspice berries over medium heat, tossing constantly, until just fragrant, about 2 minutes. Add the vinegar, sugar, and salt and bring to a boil, stirring to dissolve. Remove the pan from heat and stir in the bay leaf, oregano, orange zest strips, orange juice, lime juice, and garlic. Let cool slightly.

3. Pour the brine over the vegetables to cover. Seal the container and let it sit at room temperature for at least 3 hours and up to 3 days. Taste it every day to see how the flavor develops as it sits, and when it's to your liking (but no longer than 3 days, this isn't intended to be a long ferment), move to the fridge and store for up to 3 months.

SWAP CORNER

I love the combination of allspice and peppercorn for a hint of warmth and nutty heat, especially with sunny orange zest. I use these because they grow in Mexico and remind me of the flavors of mole and guisos (stews). But you should use the spices and citrus you're drawn to. Caraway, celery seeds, cumin seeds, fennel seeds, lemon zest in place of orange? All great. Just match the volume measurement, because a little goes a long way.

Grilled sausage sandwiches

Bloody Marias

VACIAR EL REFRI CHILES ENCURTIDOS

EMPTY-THE-FRIDGE PICKLED CHILES
Chiles of your choice, coriander, and star anise

You know who you are. You have three types of pickled hot peppers in your fridge door at all times, and I see you. That briny heat makes everything better, plus you can chop up the chiles and mix them in sour cream or mayo for a quick dip or spread—versatility! This recipe is how I use up the random chiles in my crisper at the end of the week, chopping them lengthwise in quarters to mimic pickle spears (but you can do round slices if you prefer).

MAKES 1 QUART/LITER

- 1 cup distilled white, apple cider, or another 5% acidity vinegar
- 1 tablespoon coriander seeds (or your faves! Have fun!)
- 2 fresh or dried bay leaves
- 1 whole clove
- ½ star anise pod (if you love it, use the whole pod)
- 4½ teaspoons Diamond Crystal kosher salt (0.7 oz/20 g)
- 14.1 ounces (400 g) fresh chiles of your choice, rinsed, stemmed, halved, quartered, or sliced (I used 4 chiles jalapeños and 6 chiles güeros)
- 3 garlic cloves, peeled and smashed (but still holding their shape)
- 2 tablespoons extra-virgin olive oil

SPECIAL EQUIPMENT

1-quart/liter nonreactive container with a lid. Glass, ceramic, stainless steel, food-grade plastic, and silicone will all work.

SERVING SUGGESTIONS

Chop up and add to softened cream cheese for a sandwich spread; add to cornbread or biscuits; top burgers, pizza, and the usual suspects.

1. In a medium saucepan, combine 1 cup water, the vinegar, coriander seeds, bay leaves, clove, star anise, and salt and bring to a boil over high heat. Remove from the heat and let sit for 5 minutes to cool slightly.

2. Meanwhile, stuff the chiles and garlic into a 1-quart/liter nonreactive container with a lid. The chiles will be packed in and that is okay.

3. Pour the hot vinegar mixture over the chiles to cover. If the tops of your chiles are above the vinegar, add a tablespoon or two of vinegar and water to cover, but allow about ½ inch of room from the top of the jar.

4. Top with the olive oil, seal the container, and let sit at room temperature for at least 3 hours, and up to 3 days. Taste every day to see how the flavor develops as it sits, and when it's to your liking (but no longer than 3 days, this isn't intended to be a long ferment), move it to the fridge and store for up to 6 months.

WHAT'S WITH THE OLIVE OIL?
It creates a barrier. Since we're not using fermentation weights here, the olive oil (or any oil) is the barrier that keeps air off the surface of the brine—and therefore keeping bacterial growth at bay. It also imparts some nice flavor. That's all to say: Don't skip it.

SALSA JARDINERA ESTILO MEXICANA

MEXICAN-STYLE GIARDINIERA
Cauliflower, poblano, and chiltepín

Inspired by the memory of eating an entire moon-size muffuletta from Central Grocery in New Orleans (washed down with a can of Coke), I wanted to make a giardiniera-style mix with some Mexican flavors: poblano, serrano, Mexican oregano. Use it piled onto every sandwich, burger, and hot dog in sight. Or tacos! Duh. The vegetables become crisp-tender and as they gently ferment, they become more garlicky, the poblano gets plump and juicy, and the brine nicely spicy. I can eat it by the bowlful.

MAKES 2 QUARTS/LITERS

- ¼ head cauliflower (10.5 oz/300 g), cored and chopped into florets
- 2 medium carrots (7.8 oz/221 g), chopped
- 1 large chile poblano (5.2 oz/148 g), stemmed, seeded, and chopped
- 3 celery stalks (4.4 oz/126 g), ends trimmed and chopped
- 4 chiles serranos (2.7 oz/76 g), stemmed and sliced
- ¼ cup (1.7 oz/48 g) plus 1½ teaspoons (0.2 oz/6 g) Diamond Crystal kosher salt
- 2 teaspoons dried oregano, preferably Mexican
- 2 teaspoons coriander seeds
- ½ teaspoon cumin seeds
- 2 tablespoons chiles chiltepín (0.4 oz/10 g) or 10 chiles de árbol
- 2 avocado leaves or bay leaves
- 6 garlic cloves, peeled and smashed
- 2 cups white wine vinegar
- 4 tablespoons extra-virgin olive oil

SPECIAL EQUIPMENT

Two 1-quart/liter nonreactive containers with a lid. Glass, ceramic, stainless steel, food-grade plastic, and silicone will all work.

SERVING SUGGESTIONS

Sandwiches, hot dogs, chicken salad.

1. In a large bowl, combine the cauliflower, carrots, poblano, celery, serranos, and ¼ cup of the salt (1.7 oz/48 g). Add water to cover (about 8 cups) and stir until the salt has dissolved. Cover the bowl and let sit at room temperature for at least 6 hours and up to 12. The vegetables will soften slightly and release water as they sit, which will allow them to soak up the flavors of the brine better.

2. Drain and rinse the vegetables to remove excess salt. Set aside until ready to use.

3. In a small bowl, stir together the oregano, coriander, cumin, chiles, avocado leaves, and garlic until combined. Divide the spice mixture between two 1-quart/liter nonreactive containers with lids.

4. In a medium saucepan, combine 2 cups water, the vinegar, and remaining 1½ teaspoons salt (0.2 oz/6 g) and bring to a boil over high heat. Remove from the heat and let sit for 5 minutes to cool slightly.

5. Meanwhile, stuff the reserved vegetables into the spice-filled jars. Pour the hot vinegar mixture over the vegetables to cover. If anything is poking out above the vinegar, add a tablespoon or two of vinegar and water to cover, but allow about ½ inch of room from the top of the jar.

6. Top each jar with 2 tablespoons of the olive oil, seal the container, and let sit at room temperature for at least 24 hours and up to 4 days. Taste every day to see how the flavor develops as it sits, and when it's to your liking (but no longer than 4 days, this isn't intended to be a long ferment), move to the fridge and store for up to 1 month.

SONORAN-STYLE HOT DOGS
PAGE 275

SALSA PICANTE DE JALAPEÑO

JALAPEÑO HOT SAUCE
Jalapeño, onion, and olive oil

I either have this, or the Salsa Picante de Valentina (page 156), in my fridge at all times. (Salsa emergencies have been eliminated in this house.) Just sautéing the jalapeños and onion alone will make you want to stop right then and serve that over everything—the smell is incredible—but keep going. It's thicker than your average salsa picante, but don't let that stop you from soaking it into everything, from burgers to tacos. The flavor is savory and tangy, a lot less hot than my dad's jalapeño salsa (see page 57), with a toasty golden-brown note from the seared ingredients.

MAKES 3 CUPS

- 3 tablespoons extra-virgin olive oil
- 8 chiles jalapeños (1 lb/469 g), stemmed and roughly chopped
- ¼ medium onion (4 oz/112 g), roughly chopped
- 3 garlic cloves, peeled and smashed (but still holding their shape)
- 2 teaspoons Diamond Crystal kosher salt (0.28 oz/8 g), plus more to taste
- ½ cup distilled white vinegar, plus more to taste

SPECIAL EQUIPMENT

1-pint (500 ml) nonreactive container with a lid. Glass, ceramic, stainless steel, food-grade plastic, and silicone will all work.

SERVING SUGGESTIONS

Any taco, especially eggs and chorizo; platters of nachos or with chips.

1. In a medium skillet, heat the oil over medium-high. Add the jalapeños, onion, garlic, and salt and cook, stirring occasionally, until the edges of the onion are just beginning to turn brown, 8 to 10 minutes.

2. Add 1 cup water and bring to a boil, scraping up any browned bits off the bottom of the skillet, and cook until the jalapeños are tender, about 5 minutes.

3. Add the vinegar, bring to a boil, and remove from the heat. Let cool for 5 minutes.

4. Transfer the chile mixture and cooking liquid to a blender and carefully purée until smooth. Taste and season with more salt or vinegar if desired. Let cool.

5. Using a funnel, pour into a hot sauce bottle or a 1-pint (500 ml) nonreactive container with a lid. Seal the container and let sit at room temperature for at least 3 hours, and up to 4 days. Taste every day to see how the flavor develops as it sits, and when it's to your liking (but no longer than 4 days, this isn't intended to be a long ferment), move to the fridge and store for up to 6 months.

• Tostilocos

Jicama, cucumber, and mango

Seafood ceviche

SALSA PICANTE DE VALENTINA

VALENTINA HOT SAUCE
Puya, serrano, and garlic

Now it's time for a true fermented hot sauce. That doesn't mean more work, it just means time. The reward is a sauce with a much more interesting, enticing flavor. Valentina, which is basically the national hot sauce of Mexico, is not fermented (much), but I love it and wanted to imagine a homemade version that brings a little more funk to the party. Because we're not using thickeners, preservatives, or stabilizers, the sauce won't be as silky smooth as the jarred version, but it should coat the back of the spoon, or trace along the beer glass you're making a Michelada in . . .

MAKES 2 CUPS

- 24 chiles puyas (1 oz/30 g) or 4 chiles guajillos, stemmed and seeded
- 23 chiles secos/dried serranos (0.7 oz/20 g) or 20 dried chiles de árbol, stemmed and seeded
- 3 garlic cloves (0.5 oz/17 g), peeled and smashed (but still holding their shape)
- ¼ teaspoon cumin seeds
- ½ teaspoon dried oregano, preferably Mexican
- 1 dried bay leaf
- 1 ounce (29 g) sea salt (not iodized!)
- 22.5 ounces (640 g) water, preferably spring, filtered and/or nonchlorinated, not tap! (See "Why Sea Salt? Why Not Tap Water?," opposite)

SPECIAL EQUIPMENT

One 1-quart/liter canning jar with lid (like a Ball jar); glass or ceramic fermentation weight—all dishwasher-clean

SERVING SUGGESTIONS

Everything.

1. In a 1-quart/liter canning jar with lid, combine the puyas, serranos, garlic, cumin seeds, oregano, bay leaf, and sea salt. Pour the water over to cover. Seal the jar and shake vigorously for 1 minute to dissolve the salt. Top with a glass or ceramic fermentation weight (or a small jar/ramekin partially filled with water) to keep the chiles and garlic fully submerged in the brine. Loosely secure the lid and store in a dark, cool (room-temperature) place, where it will live for 4 weeks.

2. After 72 hours, you will see bubbles floating up the jar, like a flute of champagne. It's time to burp the jar. Open the lid and release the gasses, and make sure everything is still submerged below the brine (if it's not, put on gloves and push them under, rearranging the weight as needed). Leuconostoc bacteria are now thriving and producing carbon dioxide. It will smell really delicious, like a mild kimchi.

3. DAYS 4 THROUGH 10: Keep burping until you stop seeing bubbles, around day 10. (If it smells like death, something wasn't clean, there wasn't enough salt, or it was stored in too warm a place. Sorry, but toss it!) Around day 6, the bubbles will have decreased and the brine will become cloudy and start to smell pleasantly sour. *Lactobacillus* is now thriving and producing lactic acid. Once the bubbles are gone, you don't need to burp the baby anymore.

4. DAYS 10 TO 30: As the lactic acid increases, the sourness increases and the chiles will become fully preserved. Continue to check the progress by opening the lid and smelling. Taste with a clean spoon. Just don't put any half-eaten anything back in the jar, and no double-dipping!

Why Sea Salt?
Why Not Tap Water?

Salt in a fermented hot sauce isn't just enhancing flavor, it's inhibiting bad bacterial growth. We want to use the least processed salt—so, *not* iodized—with nothing added to it that would inhibit the good bacteria from growing, too. Ditto the water. Tap water is often treated with chlorine or fluoride that will kill the good bacteria that are fueling the fermentation. You'd need to let tap water sit out in a bowl for a few hours for the chlorine to evaporate to use it, so I make life easier and use filtered instead.

5. AROUND DAY 30: Remove the lid, remove and discard anything floating on the surface. (White or even blue mold is common, so don't get scared; scoop it out and discard. Black or other colors of mold, though, not good, sorry—toss it all.) Wear gloves to remove the weight, and smell and taste the brine with a clean spoon. At this point they should be ready to blend and eat. But everyone has their flavor preference. If you want a more sour flavor, put the weight back in the jar and submerge everything, seal the jar, and continue to ferment in a cool, dark place, tasting every 2 or 3 days until it's at the acidity you like. The flavor and acidity will continue to develop as it ferments, up to about day 50.

6. When they are at the acidity you like, drain the chiles in a fine-mesh sieve and reserve the fermenting liquid. Transfer all the solids to a blender, add 1¼ cups of the fermenting liquid and purée until completely smooth. Thin with more fermenting liquid if desired (or water, if the brine is too sour for you) and transfer to a clean jar or hot sauce bottle and refrigerate. Hot sauce is most flavorful within 6 months.

MICHELADA LIKE YOU MEAN IT
Rub a wedge of lime around the rim of a pint glass and dip in salt (or Tajín). Pour in a Mexican lager, a dash of this hot sauce, a dash of Worcestershire, and a good squeeze of lime. Stir and drink.

SALSA PICANTE DE PIÑA

PINEAPPLE HOT SAUCE
Pineapple, habanero, and ginger

You might recognize this one because there's a fresh salsa version of this hot sauce on page 44. (Make both, see what happens!) Same ingredients, completely different formats. The pineapple and habanero are a dream together, making a sweet-sour, funky sauce that gives off the vaguest hint of beer the way tepache (a low-alcohol, 24-hour fermented pineapple drink) does. A little clove and ginger bring unexpected back notes of my favorite spices, but you can play around with peppercorns, star anise, or skip the ginger entirely to let the pineapple sweetness shine.

MAKES 2 CUPS

- 12.3 ounces (350 g) pineapple (about ¼ large), peeled, cored, and sliced
- 3 chiles habaneros (0.9 oz/26 g), stemmed, halved, and seeded
- 3 garlic cloves (0.5 oz/16 g), peeled and smashed (but still holding their shape)
- 0.3 ounce (9 g) grated fresh ginger (about ½-inch knob)
- 1 whole clove
- 1 ounce (30 g) sea salt (not iodized!)
- 13 ounces (370 g) water, preferably, spring, filtered and/or non-chlorinated, not tap! (See "Why Sea Salt? Why Not Tap Water?," page 157)

SPECIAL EQUIPMENT

One 1-quart/liter canning jar with lid (like a Ball jar); glass or ceramic fermentation weight—all dishwasher-clean

1. In a 1-quart/liter canning jar with lid, combine the pineapple, habaneros, garlic, ginger, clove, and salt. Pour the water over to cover. Seal the jar and shake vigorously for 2 minutes to dissolve the salt and release some of the liquid in the pineapple. Top with a glass or ceramic fermentation weight (or small jar/ramekin partially filled with water) to keep everything fully submerged in the brine. Loosely secure the lid and store in a dark, cool (room temperature) place, where it will live for 4 weeks.

2. After 72 hours, you will see bubbles floating up the jar, like a flute of champagne. It's time to burp the jar. Open the lid and release the gasses, and make sure everything is still submerged below the brine (if it's not, put on gloves and push them under and rearrange the weight as needed). Leuconostoc bacteria are now thriving and producing carbon dioxide. It will smell really delicious, like a mild kombucha.

3. DAYS 4 THROUGH 10: Keep burping until you stop seeing bubbles, around day 10. (If it smells like death, something wasn't clean, there wasn't enough salt, or it was stored in too warm a place—Sorry, but toss it!) Around day 6, the bubbles will have decreased and the brine will become cloudy and start to smell pleasantly sour. *Lactobacillus* are now thriving and producing lactic acid. Once the bubbles are gone, you don't need to burp the baby anymore.

4. DAYS 10 TO 30: As the lactic acid increases, the sourness increases and the chiles will become fully preserved. Continue to check the progress by opening the lid and smelling. Taste with a clean spoon. Just don't put any half-eaten anything back in the jar, and no double-dipping!

5. AROUND DAY 30: Remove the lid, remove and discard anything floating on the surface. (White or even blue mold is common so don't get scared; scoop it out and discard. Black or other colors of mold, though, not good, sorry—toss the jar.) Wear gloves to remove the weight, and smell and taste the brine with a clean spoon. At this point they should be ready to blend and eat. But everyone has their flavor preference. If you want a more sour flavor, put the weight back in the jar and submerge everything, seal the jar, and continue to ferment in a cool, dark place, tasting every 2 or 3 days until it's at the acidity you like. The flavor and acidity will continue to develop as it ferments, up to about day 50.

6. When they are at the acidity you like, drain the pineapple and chiles in a fine-mesh sieve and reserve the fermenting liquid. Transfer all the solids to a blender, add 1 cup of the fermenting liquid and purée until completely smooth. Thin with more fermenting liquid if desired (or water, if the brine is too sour for you) and transfer to a clean jar or hot sauce bottle and refrigerate. Hot sauce is most flavorful within 6 months.

● Pepperoni and mushroom pizza

CHILES LACTO-FERMENTADOS

LACTO-FERMENTED CHILES
Chiles, sea salt, and water

When I was working in the test kitchen of *Bon Appétit,* I loved working with Joe Beddia on recipes from his great book *Pizza Camp.* His fermented chiles on pizza have a fresh, more zesty-tart taste than the ones you buy in jars, and it started my love affair with fermentation. Now, his recipe only ferments for 48 hours. But, by taking a full month like we do here, the flavor becomes more complex, less acidic than vinegar pickles, and more savory, like you dropped a pinch of MSG in the jar. These chiles are fantastic on pizza, obviously, but try them chopped up in cheddar biscuits or cornbread, too.

MAKES 1 QUART/LITER

- 12 ounces (340 g) fresh chiles of your choice (I used serranos), thinly sliced
- 3 garlic cloves (0.5 oz/16 g), peeled and smashed (but still holding their shape)
- 1 ounce (30 g) sea salt (not iodized!)
- 14 ounces (400 g) water, preferably, spring, filtered and/or non-chlorinated, not tap! (See "Why Sea Salt? Why Not Tap Water?," page 157)

SPECIAL EQUIPMENT

One 1-quart/liter canning jar with lid (like a Ball jar); glass or ceramic fermentation weight—all dishwasher-clean

SERVING SUGGESTIONS

Pizza, come on!

1. In a 1-quart/liter canning jar with lid, combine the chiles, garlic, and salt. Pour the water over to cover. Seal the jar and shake vigorously for 2 minutes to dissolve the salt and release some of the liquid in the chiles and garlic. Top with a glass or ceramic fermentation weight (or small jar/ramekin partially filled with water) to keep chiles and garlic fully submerged in the brine. Loosely secure the lid and store in a dark, cool (room temperature) place, where it will live for 4 weeks.

2. After 72 hours you will see bubbles floating up the jar, like a flute of champagne. It's time to burp the jar. Open the lid and release the gasses, and make sure everything is still submerged below the brine (if it's not, put on gloves and push them under and rearrange the weight as needed). Leuconostoc bacteria are now thriving and producing carbon dioxide. It will smell really delicious, like a mild kombucha.

3. DAYS 4 THROUGH 10: Keep burping until you stop seeing bubbles, around day 10. (If it smells like death, something wasn't clean, there wasn't enough salt, or it was stored in too warm a place—Sorry, but toss it!) Around day 6, the bubbles will have decreased and the brine will become cloudy and start to smell pleasantly sour. *Lactobacillus* is now thriving and producing lactic acid. Once the bubbles are gone, you don't need to burp the baby anymore.

4. DAYS 10 TO 30: As the lactic acid increases, the sourness increases and the chiles will become fully preserved. Continue to check the progress by opening the lid and smelling. Taste with a clean spoon. Just don't put any half-eaten anything back in the jar, and no double-dipping!

5. AROUND DAY 30: Remove the lid, remove and discard anything floating on the surface. (White or even blue mold is common so don't get scared; scoop it out and discard. Black or other colors of mold, though, not good, sorry—toss the jar.) Wear gloves to remove the weight, and smell and taste the chiles with a clean spoon! At this point they should be ready to eat. But as with a good steak, everyone has their flavor preference. If you taste the chiles but want a more sour flavor, put the weight back in the jar and submerge all the chiles, seal the jar, and continue to ferment in a cool, dark place, tasting every 2 to 3 days until they are at the acidity you like. The flavor and acidity will continue to develop as they ferment up to about day 45.

6. Store in an airtight container in the refrigerator. Chiles are most flavorful within 6 months.

SALSA FOR

SIETE

FOOD

☀️ This book is packed with salsas that are beautiful with seafood, but there's one that reigns: Salsa Bruja (Witches' Salsa, page 166). This is a spicy vinegar salsa that, as you may have guessed from the name, is witchy hot. Unlike the other pickles in this chapter, this salsa is all about the *brine,* not the veg, which is there to infuse the vinegar. This is another way the definition of salsa reveals itself to mean many, many things. You dip your spoon into the vinegar atop the pickled veg and drizzle it all over your fried fish (as you would malt vinegar with fish and chips) or any fried seafood, or use it as a mignonette with oysters, mixed with mayo for tartar sauce, in a Bloody Mary, or even as the vinegar in a salad vinaigrette. And don't forget the veg! Chop 'em up and put in that taco. Mix into that tartar. Or throw them into your Bloody Mary, too.

SALSA BRUJA

WITCHES' SALSA
Guajillo, rosemary, and vinegar

MAKES 1 QUART/LITER

- 1½ cups apple cider vinegar
- 4 large chiles guajillos (1.4 oz/40 g), stemmed and seeded
- 24 fresh or dried chiles de árbol (0.8 oz/24 g), stemmed
- 4½ teaspoons Diamond Crystal kosher salt (0.6 oz/18 g)
- 3 dried bay leaves
- 2 fresh thyme sprigs
- 1 fresh rosemary sprig
- 1 teaspoon allspice berries
- 1 whole clove
- ¼ medium red onion (4 oz/112 g), sliced
- 1 medium carrot (3.8 oz/110 g), cut into sticks
- 2 celery stalks (3 oz/84 g), ends trimmed, cut into sticks
- 2 chiles serranos (1.3 oz/38 g), stemmed and sliced lengthwise into sticks
- 3 garlic cloves, peeled and smashed (but still holding their shape)

SPECIAL EQUIPMENT

1-quart/liter nonreactive container with a lid. Glass, ceramic, stainless steel, food-grade plastic, and silicone will all work.

1. In a medium saucepan, combine 1½ cups water, the vinegar, guajillos, chiles de árbol, salt, bay leaves, thyme, rosemary, allspice, and clove and bring to a boil. Cover, reduce to a simmer, and cook for 5 minutes. Remove from the heat and let sit for 10 minutes, until the chiles are very soft. (Why are we boiling the chiles? See page 18.)

2. Meanwhile, stuff the onion, carrot, celery, serranos, and garlic into a 1-quart/liter nonreactive container with a lid.

3. Pour the warm brine over the vegetables to cover. Seal the container and let sit at room temperature for at least 3 hours and up to 3 days. Flavors will develop as it sits, so taste until it's to your liking.

4. After that, refrigerate for up to 6 months.

Fried seafood

COCTEL DE CAMARÓN

SHRIMP COCKTAIL
Poached shrimp, salsa bruja,
and ketchup

In Mexico, shrimp cocktail is more of a main dish than an appetizer. It's served in a big goblet full of a cocktail sauce that combines pico de gallo, Salsa Bruja (page 166), and hot sauce, ready to be spooned over endless tostadas. Who doesn't want that? (Some add a splash of orange soda like Fanta, but I just can't.) Ideally, you're eating this on the beach, but I'll let you take it from here.

SERVES 4

Diamond Crystal kosher salt

1 teaspoon granulated sugar (0.14 oz/4 g)

1 pound (453 g) jumbo or large shrimp, peeled and deveined

2 medium Roma tomatoes (8.6 oz/246 g), chopped

½ large cucumber (7.5 oz/214 g), chopped

½ medium red onion (6.3 oz/178 g), chopped

2 chiles serranos (0.7 oz/21 g), stemmed and chopped

⅓ cup ketchup

2 tablespoons fresh orange juice (or fine, a splash of Fanta)

1 tablespoon fresh lime juice

1 tablespoon brine from Salsa Bruja (page 166), plus more to taste

1 tablespoon hot sauce, plus more to taste

2 tablespoons chopped fresh cilantro leaves and tender stems (0.3 oz/8 g)

1 teaspoon finely grated lime zest

1 teaspoon freshly ground black pepper

FOR SERVING

- 1 avocado, peeled, seeded, and chopped
- Tostadas (page 113)
- Saltine crackers

1. Fill a medium bowl with ice and pour in enough water to cover. Set the ice bath aside until the shrimp are cooked.

2. In a medium saucepan, bring 4 cups water, 2 tablespoons salt (0.8 oz/24 g), and the sugar to a boil over high heat. Remove from the heat, add the shrimp, and cover. Let it sit and poach in the residual heat for 3 minutes. Using a slotted spoon or spider, transfer the shrimp to the ice bath. Let sit in the ice bath for 10 minutes to cool. Remove from the ice bath, transfer to a large plate and pat dry.

3. Meanwhile, in a large bowl, toss together the tomatoes, cucumber, onion, serranos, cilantro, ketchup, orange juice, lime juice, Salsa Bruja brine, and the hot sauce until completely combined. Add the shrimp, cilantro, lime zest, and black pepper and stir to combine.

4. **TO SERVE:** Divide the shrimp cocktail among footed beer or wine goblets, a coconut shell if you are feeling fancy, or a bowl if you can't be bothered. Top each with some avocado and serve with tostadas and saltines.

6-

COOKED
SALSAS

COCI

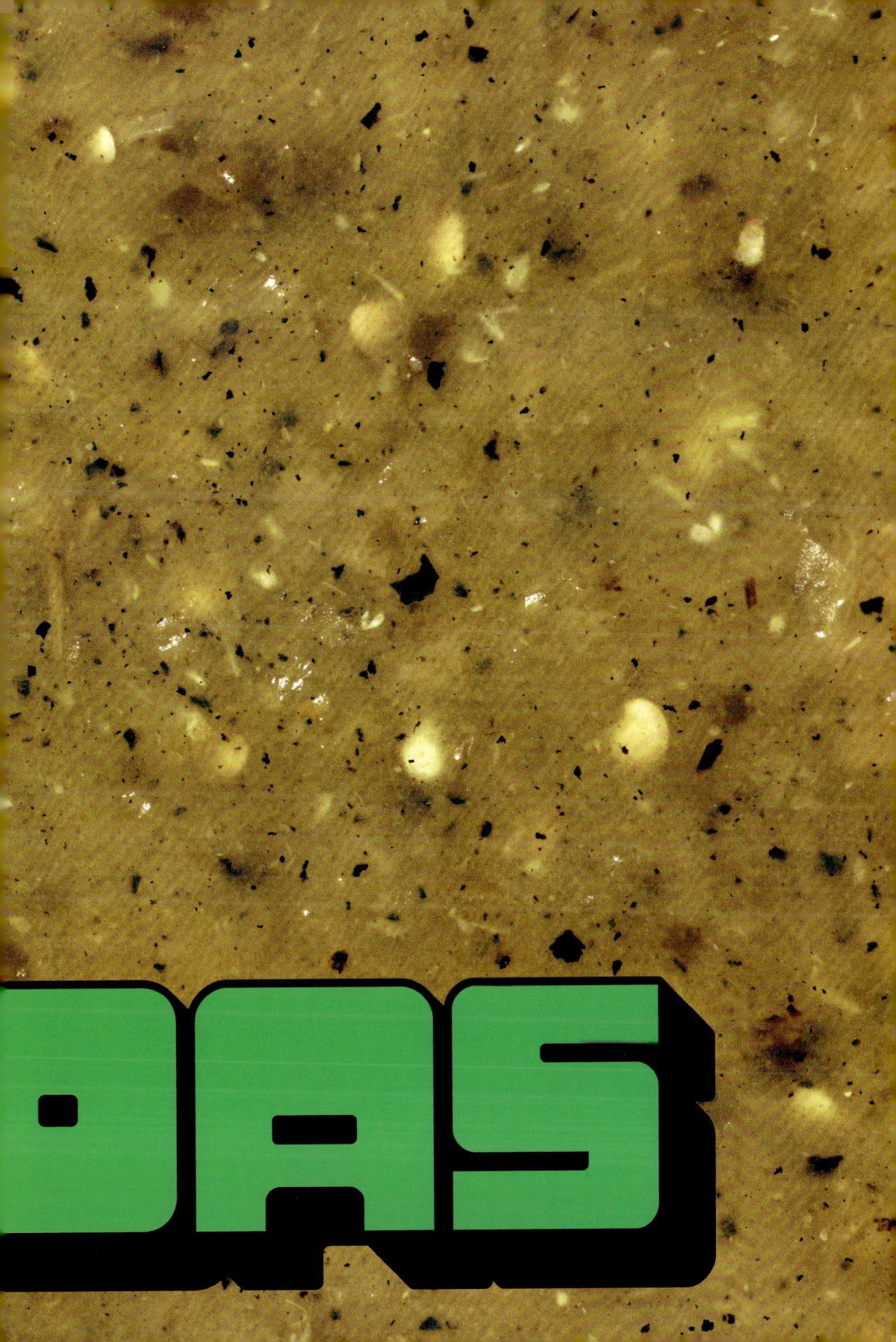

COCIDAS
—COOKED SALSAS

The previous chapters have been mostly salsas de mesa—table salsas to dip chips in, a condiment for tacos, tortas, etc. We've been there. We've done that. But salsa also means sauce, and that's what we're up to now. The first three recipes are iconic Mexican cooked salsas with a shorter ingredient list. They're easy, inexpensive, and I really just want you to get hooked on the Mole Sencillo (page 178) as much as I am. Then we'll move into the enchilada and chilaquiles salsas that pair with the full-meal recipes in Chapter 8, Comida Fácil. These are salsas to decorate dishes as you'd accessorize an outfit. Are you making the cheesy, rich Enchiladas Gratinadas on page 237? I'd dress that with a bright and happy Salsa Suiza (page 191). Are you doing Mexican-style chicken enchiladas? The iconic Salsa Guajillo (page 184) goes with everything. Think of this chapter as your dream closet, and pull recipes from it to match your mood, the season, or hell, whatever you're wearing. I've said it before and I'll say it again: There are no rules in Salsa Land.

A Quart of Salsa??
Many of the recipes here make a quart or more. It's a lot, because I make Enchiladas (page 234) or Chilaquiles (page 239) when I have random stale tortillas, so I like to keep a stash of salsa to make life easier. If you don't use it all in a few days, freeze the rest! If you have a few shreds of cheese, old tortillas, a drumstick or sausage, you're halfway to dinner if there's salsa in the freezer.

SALSA AL PASTOR

SHEPHERD'S SALSA
Guajillo, orange juice, and achiote paste

Everybody loves tacos al pastor, but I think it's even better with chicken. I've made this recipe on the road for so many food events because it always hits. There's a marinated and roasted pollo al pastor recipe in *Mi Cocina,* and this is the shortcut version for when don't have time to marinate. It's sweet, smoky, and spicy from achiote paste (a mixture of annatto seeds and spices), giving whatever you put it on a marinated, long-cooked flavor. Toss it with shredded rotisserie chicken or serve it with grilled pork or even roasted cauliflower steaks. The point is that it's instant and delicious. And it's always here for you.

MAKES 1½ CUPS

- 3 large chiles guajillos (1.5 oz/42 g), stemmed and seeded
- 3 chiles moritas (0.5 oz/13 g), stemmed
- 3 garlic cloves, peeled and smashed (but still holding their shape)
- ¾ cup low-sodium chicken stock
- ⅓ cup fresh orange juice
- 3 tablespoons achiote (annatto) paste (1.8 oz/52 g)
- 2 whole cloves
- 1 tablespoon agave syrup (preferably dark), molasses, or honey
- 1½ teaspoons Diamond Crystal kosher salt (0.2 oz/6 g), plus more to taste

SERVING SUGGESTIONS

Toss with shredded cooked chicken, pork, beef, or grilled veg. Or rub onto raw chicken, pork, beef, shrimp, fish, or veg before grilling, pan-searing, or roasting. Use as a barbecue sauce and toss with cooked meat/veg before serving.

1. In a large saucepan, combine the guajillos, moritas, garlic, chicken stock, orange juice, achiote paste, cloves, agave, and salt and bring to a boil over high heat. Cover, reduce to a simmer, and cook for 5 minutes. Remove from the heat and let sit for 10 minutes, until the chiles are very soft. (Why are we boiling the chiles? See page 18.)

2. Transfer to a blender and purée until completely smooth. Taste and season with more salt if desired.

Do ahead: The salsa can be made up to 3 days ahead. Store in an airtight container in the refrigerator, or freeze for up to 3 months.

THERE'S NO SWAP FOR ACHIOTE
The fragrant annatto and spice mixture in achiote paste is so specific, there are no alternatives. But you can definitely buy it online (usually a yellow box by La Anita or El Yucateco), or your nearest Mexican grocer, or maybe even the international aisle of the grocery store. It'll last longer than our time on this planet, so stock up and freeze any leftovers.

Tacos al pastor

Roast chicken

GREAT ON
**ENCHILADAS
&
CHILAQUILES**

PIPIÁN VERDE

GREEN NUT AND SEED SAUCE
Pepitas, peanuts, and tomatillo

Pipián, like mole, is an ancient Mexican salsa that can be green, white, or red (like the flag), and I couldn't write this book without it. Pipián is often made with crushed pumpkin seeds and chiles, herbs, and spices. It tastes substantial and important. My grandparents made a red version with chiles anchos, guajillos, Texas pecans, and peanuts. That memory inspired this recipe, with pepitas and fatty peanuts to add richness to the mild pepita. Then we've got poblanos and jalapeños for a little kick and a piquant green chile without a crazy burn. Pour it on roast chicken forever and ever.

MAKES 1½ QUARTS

- ½ cup peanuts (2.4 oz/68 g)
- 4 tablespoons extra-virgin olive oil, divided
- 1 cup pepitas/raw pumpkin seeds (5.6 oz/160 g)
- 3 medium chiles poblanos (14 oz/402 g), stemmed, seeded, and roughly chopped
- 5 medium tomatillos (8.6 oz/245 g), husked, rinsed, and quartered
- ¼ medium white onion (3.5 oz/100 g), roughly chopped
- 2 chiles jalapeños (2.3 oz/66 g), stemmed and roughly chopped
- 3 garlic cloves, peeled and smashed (but still holding their shape)
- 2½ teaspoons Diamond Crystal kosher salt (0.35 oz/10 g), plus more to taste
- 3 fresh or dried bay leaves
- ½ teaspoon dried thyme or 1 teaspoon fresh thyme leaves
- 3 cups low-sodium vegetable or chicken broth (or water)

SERVING SUGGESTIONS

Chilaquiles (page 239), roasted chicken, pork, beef, veggies, fish, shellfish, rice, Enchiladas (page 234).

1. In a large dry saucepan, toast the peanuts over medium-high heat, tossing frequently, until very fragrant and lightly browned, about 3 minutes. Transfer to a small heatproof bowl and let cool, setting aside until ready to use.

2. Add 1 tablespoon of the oil to the same pan and heat over medium-high. Add the pepitas and cook, stirring frequently to coat them (the oil will prevent them from jumping out of the pan), until they're golden brown in spots, 2 to 3 minutes. Transfer to the bowl with the peanuts.

3. Add the remaining 3 tablespoons oil to the pan and heat over medium-high. Add the poblanos, tomatillos, onion, jalapeños, garlic, and salt and cook, stirring occasionally, until the tomatillos are olive green and the poblanos are soft, 10 to 12 minutes.

4. Add the bay leaves, thyme, and broth and use a spoon to scrape up any browned bits from the bottom of the pan. Transfer the tomatillo mixture with the broth to a blender. Add the toasted pepitas and peanuts and purée until completely smooth. This could take a minute or two at high speed.

5. Using a paper towel, wipe the saucepan clean and pour the puréed salsa back into the pan. Set over medium-high heat and bring to a boil. Reduce to a simmer and cook until the salsa has thickened to the consistency of creamy gravy, about 15 minutes. Taste and season with more salt if desired.

Do ahead: The salsa can be made up to 3 days ahead. Store in an airtight container in the refrigerator, or freeze for up to 3 months.

MOLE SENCILLO

SIMPLE MOLE
Ancho, animal crackers, almonds, and chocolate

May we all strive to be as beautiful and complex as mole. It's the most famous salsa in Mexico, with a smoky-sweet-hot flavor, velvety smooth texture, and deep, striking color. It's usually a special-occasion dish because it requires a lot of time and ingredients. Not this one. I created a simple mole with only 10 ingredients (if you don't count the oil, salt, and water) and a handful of steps. It's a starter mole to help you master the same techniques used in 54-ingredient moles. It's surprisingly complex and yields a lot, so make sure to freeze a cup or two for your lucky future self.

MAKES 5 CUPS

- 1 medium Roma tomato (4.3 oz/123 g), cored but left whole
- ¼ medium white onion (3.1 oz/89 g)
- 5 tablespoons rendered lard or vegetable oil, divided
- 4 large chiles anchos (2.5 oz/72 g), stemmed and seeded
- ⅓ cup animal crackers (0.7 oz/22 g)
- ¼ cup raw almonds (1.4 oz/40 g)
- ¼ cup raisins (1.2 oz/35 g)
- 1 tablespoon raw sesame seeds (0.3 oz/10 g)
- 1 whole star anise or 1 whole clove
- 2 tablespoons Diamond Crystal kosher salt (0.8 oz/24 g), plus more to taste
- 1 tablespoon grated piloncillo or dark brown sugar (0.4 oz/13 g), plus more to taste
- 4 cups water (or low-sodium chicken stock for a richer flavor)
- 1¼ ounces (35 g) bittersweet chocolate (75% or more cacao), chopped

FOR SERVING

- Toasted sesame seeds

SERVING SUGGESTIONS

Over roasted meats, over roasted fall/winter veggies, with Enchiladas/ Enmoladas (page 234).

1. Line a medium cast-iron skillet with a sheet of foil and heat over high until very hot, about 2 minutes. Add the tomato and onion and cook, using tongs to turn occasionally, until everything is charred on all sides, 6 to 8 minutes for the onion, 8 to 10 minutes for the tomato. (Alternatively, arrange an oven rack in the top position and preheat the broiler to high. Arrange the vegetables on a foil-lined sheet pan and roast under the broiler, turning occasionally, until all sides are charred.) Transfer to a medium bowl.

2. In a large saucepan, heat 3 tablespoons of the lard over medium-high until very hot, about 1 minute. Working in batches, fry the anchos, turning to coat in the lard until fragrant, browned, and toasted on both sides, about 30 seconds. Transfer to the bowl with the charred vegetables.

3. Fry the animal crackers, tossing frequently, until golden brown and crispy, 1 to 2 minutes; transfer to the bowl with chiles.

4. Add the almonds, raisins, sesame seeds, and star anise to the pan and fry, stirring constantly, until the raisins puff and lighten in color and the almonds are browned, 1 to 2 minutes. Add the salt, sugar, water (or stock), chiles, animal crackers, tomato, and onion and bring to a boil. Cover, reduce to a simmer, and cook until the chiles and almonds are very tender, about 30 minutes.

5. Remove from the heat and let sit, covered, for 20 minutes to cool slightly before blending. *Continued* →

GREAT ON
ENCHILADAS
&
CHILAQUILES

Roasted
vegetables

MOLE
SENCILLO

Continued

Continued from page 178

6. Transfer the chile mixture and cooking liquid to a blender and carefully blend until completely smooth. Rinse the saucepan used to cook the chiles and wipe dry.

7. In the cleaned pot, heat the remaining 2 tablespoons lard over medium-high until very hot, about 1 minute or until you see tiny wisps of smoke. Carefully pour the blended mole into the hot lard—stand back from the pot; it will spit and sputter! Stir, scraping up any fried bits from the bottom of the pot. Reduce the heat to medium and continue cooking, stirring frequently, until the top of the mole is glossy and very thick, about 10 minutes.

8. Stir in the chocolate and remove from the heat, stirring until completely melted. Taste and season with more salt or sugar if desired.

9. Spoon the mole over whatever you're making for dinner, and top with toasted sesame seeds.

Do ahead: The mole can be made up to 3 days ahead. Store in an airtight container in the refrigerator, or freeze for up to 3 months.

SWAP CORNER
Everything is up for swapping if you stay within the weighted measurements. Try your favorite nuts and seeds (sunflower? nice). Swap the lard with a neutral oil to make it vegan. Or use 2 tostadas or a small piece of crusty bread in place of the animal crackers. The point is, you can make this mole your own.

Mercado
Pino Suárez,
Mazatlán, México

ALSO
**GREAT ON
ENCHILADAS**

CHILAQUILES
PAGE 239

SALSA VERDE TATEMADA

CHARRED GREEN SALSA
Tomatillo, serrano, jalapeño, and poblano

Everything in my life is good when I'm sitting down to eat chilaquiles with salsa verde, blue corn totopos, grilled chicken, and a fried egg. I like to char the vegetables in this salsa, so it's darker green, with little black flecks of deliciousness. The bitterness of the char balances the tartness of the tomatillos, so while I'd say you could roast all the vegetables if you didn't want to char them, that would have a different, sweeter result.

MAKES 1 QUART

- 7 medium tomatillos (15.8 oz/449 g), husked and rinsed
- 1 chile serrano (0.6 oz/18 g), stemmed
- 2 chiles jalapeños (2.3 oz/66 g), stemmed
- 3 tablespoons extra-virgin olive oil
- 2 medium chiles poblanos (9.5 oz/268 g), stemmed, seeded, and roughly chopped
- ¼ medium white onion (3.7 oz/105 g), roughly chopped
- 3 garlic cloves, peeled and smashed (but still holding their shape)
- 1 tablespoon Diamond Crystal kosher salt (0.42 oz/12 g), plus more to taste
- 2 cups low-sodium vegetable or chicken broth (or water)
- 2 teaspoons vegetable or chicken bouillon powder (optional; see page 14)

USE IN

Enchiladas (page 234), Enchiladas Gratinadas (page 237), or Chilaquiles (page 239).

1. Line a large cast-iron skillet with a sheet of foil and heat the skillet over high until very hot. I'd recommend opening the windows and turning your exhaust on high. Add the tomatillos, serrano, and jalapeños and cook, using tongs to turn occasionally, until everything is charred on all sides, 4 to 5 minutes for the chiles, 8 to 10 minutes for the tomatillos. (Alternatively, arrange an oven rack in the top position and preheat the broiler to high. Arrange the vegetables on a foil-lined sheet pan and roast, turning occasionally, until all sides are charred.) Transfer to a plate to cool.

2. Meanwhile, in a medium saucepan, heat the oil over medium-high. Add the poblanos, onion, garlic, and salt and cook, stirring occasionally, until the onion and poblanos are browned, 8 to 10 minutes.

3. Transfer the poblano mixture to a blender, making sure to scrape everything in. Add the charred tomatillo/chile mixture, the broth, and bouillon powder (if using) and purée until smooth.

4. Return the salsa to the same saucepan and bring to a boil. Reduce to a simmer and cook, stirring occasionally, until the salsa has thickened to the consistency of heavy cream, about 10 minutes. Taste and season with more salt if desired.

Do ahead: The salsa can be made up to 3 days ahead. Store in an airtight container in the refrigerator, or freeze for up to 3 months.

SALSA GUAJILLO

Guajillo, tomato, and oregano

I'm almost always on Team Verde. But I wanted to make a salsa roja that would make me question my life choices. This salsa guajillo is deep and hearty, but it's not heavy—thanks to juicy tomatoes and a single sneaky tomatillo. It's lighter and brighter than you'd expect. I made it with chilaquiles in mind (the acid balances against the earthiness of the crispy corn totopos), though it's a versatile salsa for pulled chicken sandwiches or for turning into compound butter to make shrimp scampi. I mean, come *on*.

MAKES 1 QUART

- 7 chiles guajillos (2.6 oz/76 g), stemmed and seeded
- 3 dried chiles de árbol (0.1 oz/3 g), stemmed
- 4 medium Roma tomatoes (15 oz/ 432 g), cored but left whole
- ¼ medium white onion (3.7 oz/105 g)
- 1 medium tomatillo (2.2 oz/64 g), husked and rinsed
- 3 garlic cloves, peeled and smashed (but still holding their shape)
- 3 cups low-sodium vegetable or chicken broth (or water)
- 2 teaspoons vegetable or chicken bouillon powder (optional; see page 14)
- ½ teaspoon dried oregano, preferably Mexican
- ¼ teaspoon cumin seeds or ground cumin
- 2½ teaspoons Diamond Crystal kosher salt (0.35 oz/10 g), plus more to taste

PAIR WITH

Enchiladas (page 234), Enchiladas Gratinadas (page 237), Chilaquiles (page 239).

1. Arrange a rack in the center of the oven and preheat to 350°F.

2. Arrange the guajillos and chiles de árbol on a sheet pan in an even layer and roast until the chiles are beginning to brown, are very fragrant, and smell almost like toasted nuts, about 5 minutes (you don't want to char the chiles or they'll taste bitter and burnt, just a medium toast). Remove from the oven and set aside to cool.

3. Line a large cast-iron skillet with a sheet of foil and heat the skillet over high until very hot. Add the tomatoes, onion, tomatillo, and garlic and cook, using tongs to turn occasionally, until everything is charred on all sides, about 3 minutes for the garlic, 6 to 8 minutes for the onion, and 8 to 10 minutes for the tomatoes. (Alternatively, arrange an oven rack in the top position and preheat the broiler on high. Arrange the vegetables on a foil-lined sheet pan and roast under the broiler, turning occasionally, until all sides are charred.) Transfer to a plate to cool.

4. In a large saucepan, combine the broth, guajillos, chiles de árbol, tomatoes, onion, tomatillo, garlic, bouillon (if using), oregano, cumin, and salt and bring to a boil over high heat. Cover, reduce to a gentle boil over medium-low heat, and cook for 20 minutes.

5. Carefully transfer to a blender and purée until smooth. Taste and season with more salt if desired.

Do ahead: The salsa can be made up to 3 days ahead. Store in an airtight container in the refrigerator, or freeze for up to 3 months.

TURN THIS SALSA INTO COMPOUND BUTTER
Soften a stick of butter and then mix in 2 to 4 tablespoons of salsa depending on how salsa-forward you want it to be. Roll it into a log or smash into a container and store in the fridge for scampi night.

Shrimp scampi

ALBONDIGAS
SUB
PAGE 242

GREAT ON
ENCHILADAS
&
CHILAQUILES

SALSA PARA ENTOMATADAS

ENTOMATADA SAUCE
Tomato, onion, and chile de árbol

Entomatadas are similar to enchiladas, with a gorgeous tomato sauce instead of chile (for the recipe, see page 234). This entomatada sauce is inspired by a torta I devoured in Guadalajara at Carnitas El Bigotes with a salsa that was so intense, it was almost like a thin, super-concentrated tomato water. It was bright and tangy, and smooth, but rich like a jellied stock. Mind-blowing. I like heat in all my salsas, so I added a few chiles to this recipe, but if you want pure tomato bliss, you can leave them out.

MAKES 1 QUART

- 3 tablespoons extra-virgin olive oil
- ¼ medium white onion (3.7 oz/105 g), roughly chopped
- 3 garlic cloves, peeled and smashed (but still holding their shape)
- 2½ teaspoons Diamond Crystal kosher salt (0.35 oz/10 g), plus more to taste
- 8 medium Roma tomatoes (1.8 lb/ 818 g), cored and roughly chopped
- 3 fresh or dried chiles de árbol (0.1 oz/3 g), stemmed (optional)
- 1 cup low-sodium vegetable or chicken broth (or water)
- 2 teaspoons vegetable or chicken bouillon powder (optional; see page 14)

PAIR WITH

Enchiladas (page 234), Enchiladas Gratinadas (page 237), Chilaquiles (page 239).

1. In a large saucepan, heat the oil over medium-high. Add the onion, garlic, and salt and cook, stirring occasionally, until the onion is translucent and beginning to brown, 4 to 5 minutes.

2. Add the tomatoes and chiles de árbol (if using) and cook, stirring occasionally, until the tomatoes are falling apart and most of their liquid has evaporated, about 5 minutes.

3. Transfer to a blender making sure to scrape everything in and add the broth and bouillon powder (if using) and purée until smooth.

4. Return to the same saucepan and bring to a boil over high heat. Reduce to a simmer and cook, stirring occasionally, until the salsa has thickened to the consistency of heavy cream, about 15 minutes. Taste and season with more salt if desired.

Do ahead: The salsa can be made up to 3 days ahead. Store in an airtight container in the refrigerator, or freeze for up to 3 months.

SWAP CORNER
If you can, use the best tomatoes possible. But if the store tomatoes are sad, use a 28-ounce can of peeled whole tomatoes and their juices.

SALSA COSTEÑO

FRUITS OF THE SEA SALSA
Tomato, tomatillo, and
shrimp stock

Here is a salsa that's fit for your finest shrimp: grilled, poached, boiled, or even as shrimp chilaquiles, which are so damn good. It's a tomato, tomatillo, guajillo salsa with a splash of seafood stock for a subtle back note. Frying the salsa in oil deepens its flavor and helps emulsify the sauce so its components don't separate. You can use boxed or jarred stock, but if you're already prepping shrimp for chilaquiles or enchiladas, you can use the shells to make a quick stock.

MAKES 1 QUART

- 2 medium Roma tomatoes (9.2 oz/ 261 g), cored and left whole
- 3 medium tomatillos (7.4 oz/211 g), husked and rinsed
- ¼ medium white onion (3.1 oz/89 g)
- 3 garlic cloves, peeled and smashed (but still holding their shape)
- 5 tablespoons extra-virgin olive oil, divided
- 2 cups shrimp, fish or shellfish stock (see below)
- 2 large chiles guajillos (0.8 oz/20 g), stemmed and seeded
- 4 dried chiles de árbol (0.15 oz/4 g), stemmed
- 2 fresh thyme sprigs or ½ teaspoon dried
- 1 fresh or dried bay leaf
- ½ teaspoon dried oregano, preferably Mexican
- 2½ teaspoons Diamond Crystal kosher salt (0.35 oz/10 g), plus more to taste

PAIR WITH

Enchiladas (page 234), Enchiladas Gratinadas (page 237), Chilaquiles (page 239).

1. Arrange a rack in the center of the oven and preheat to 475°F.

2. In a 13 × 9-inch baking pan, toss together the tomatoes, tomatillos, onion, garlic, and 3 tablespoons of the olive oil until completely coated.

3. Roast until the tomato and tomatillo skins are browned in spots and starting to peel away from the flesh, 30 to 35 minutes. Remove the pan from the oven and set aside to cool.

4. In a medium saucepan, bring the stock, guajillos, chiles de árbol, thyme, bay leaf, oregano, and salt to a boil over high heat. Cover, reduce to a simmer, and cook for 5 minutes. Remove from the heat and let sit for 10 minutes, until the chiles are very soft. (Why are we boiling the chiles? See page 18.)

5. Transfer the chiles and cooking liquid to a blender. Add the roasted tomatoes, tomatillos, onion, and garlic and purée until completely smooth.

6. Using a paper towel, wipe the saucepan clean. Add the remaining 2 tablespoons oil and heat over high until it is very hot. Carefully pour the salsa into the hot oil—it will spit and sputter, so wear an apron and long sleeves. Stir, scraping up any fried bits from the bottom of the pan, and cook until the salsa has darkened slightly and the bubbling has settled down, about 1 minute. Stir in the salt and remove from the heat. Taste and season with more salt if desired.

Do ahead: The salsa can be made up to 3 days ahead. Store in an airtight container in the refrigerator, or freeze for up to 3 months.

QUICK SEAFOOD STOCK
In a large pot, add the shells, heads, or tails from shrimp, crab or lobster; or the bones, head, and tail from a fish. Add 4 cups water and aromatics like shallot, garlic, and herbs. Bring to a boil and then reduce to a simmer and cook, uncovered, for 25 minutes. Strain, and voilà.

GREAT ON
**ENCHILADAS
&
CHILAQUILES**

• Clams in salsa

ALSO
GREAT ON
CHILAQUILES

ENCHILADAS
SUIZAS
PAGE 237

SALSA SUIZA

SWISS SALSA
Tomatillo, sesame, and cream

Why Swiss? This luscious enchilada sauce dates back to the end of the nineteenth century at Café Imperio in Mexico City, and the "Swiss" either refers to the fact that Switzerland was a top dairy producer, or because the enchiladas topped with melted white queso resembled snow-covered Alps. Or both! Whatever, it's delicious. The cream tames the tartness of the tomatillos, and the toasted sesame seeds add a gorgeous nutty flavor.

MAKES 6 CUPS

- 4 tablespoons extra-virgin olive oil, divided
- 6 tablespoons raw sesame seeds (2.5 oz/72 g)
- 2 tablespoons pepitas/raw pumpkin seeds (0.7 oz/20 g)
- 16 medium tomatillos (1.75 lb/784 g), husked, rinsed, and quartered
- ¼ medium white onion (3.5 oz/100 g), roughly chopped
- 3 chiles serranos (1.8 oz/50 g), stemmed and roughly chopped
- 3 garlic cloves, peeled and smashed (but still holding their shape)
- 2½ teaspoons Diamond Crystal kosher salt (0.35 oz/10 g), plus more to taste
- 1 cup low-sodium vegetable or chicken broth (or water)
- 1 cup heavy cream
- 2 teaspoons vegetable or chicken bouillon powder (optional; see page 14)

PAIR WITH

Enchiladas (page 234), Enchiladas Gratinadas (page 237), Chilaquiles (page 239).

1. In a large saucepan, heat 1 tablespoon of the oil over medium-high. Add the sesame seeds and pepitas and cook, stirring frequently to coat them (the oil will prevent them from jumping out of the pan), until the sesame seeds are golden brown, 1 to 2 minutes. Transfer to a small heatproof bowl to cool.

2. Add the remaining 3 tablespoons oil to the same pan along with the tomatillos, onion, serranos, garlic, and salt and cook, stirring occasionally, until the tomatillos are olive green and very soft, 8 to 10 minutes.

3. Add the broth and deglaze the pan, using a spoon to scrape up any browned bits from the bottom of the pan. Transfer the tomatillo mixture and the broth to a blender. Add the toasted seeds and purée until smooth.

4. Using a paper towel, wipe the saucepan clean. Pour the puréed salsa back into the pan and set over medium-high heat. Add the cream and bouillon powder (if using) and bring to a boil. Reduce to a simmer and cook until the salsa has thickened to the consistency of heavy cream, about 15 minutes. Taste and season with more salt if desired

Do ahead: The salsa can be made up to 3 days ahead. Store in an airtight container in the refrigerator, or freeze for up to 3 months.

MEXICAN VS. SPANISH MANCHEGO
Manchego cheese originated in Spain, but Mexican manchego is a big part of Mexican cuisine and is made with cow's milk instead of sheep's milk. It has a smooth and creamy texture (because it's not aged like the Spanish stuff) with a mild, nutty flavor. If you can't find it, queso Chihuahua or Monterey Jack is a good swap.

TEX-MEX ENCHILADA SAUCE

Beef, chili powder, and tomato

Tex-Mex cuisine is as valid as any other, and I love it to my core. In the 1920s and '30s, Texans called a sauce like this "chile gravy," so feel free to do so yourself. The flavor combination of ground beef and chili powder cannot be duplicated, creating a nostalgic warmth that takes me home. This recipe is inspired by my dad's enchiladas. He worked at El Patio, a Tex-Mex restaurant in Austin, when he was in high school in the 1950s (and it's still around! The enchiladas are that good).

MAKES 5 CUPS

- ¼ cup rendered lard or vegetable oil, divided
- 1 pound (453 g) ground beef, preferably chuck (20% fat)
- 2 medium Roma tomatoes (8.3 oz/236 g), cored and finely chopped
- ½ medium white onion (6.3 oz/179 g), finely chopped
- 3 garlic cloves, finely grated
- 2½ teaspoons Diamond Crystal kosher salt (0.35 oz/10 g), plus more to taste
- ½ cup chili powder
- 2 tablespoons all-purpose flour (0.6 oz/16 g)
- ½ teaspoon ground cumin
- 5 cups low-sodium chicken broth

PAIR WITH

Enchiladas (page 234), Enchiladas Gratinadas (page 237), Chilaquiles (page 239).

1. In a large skillet, heat 2 tablespoons of the lard over medium-high until very hot, about 1 minute. Add the ground beef and cook, using a wooden spoon to break up any clumps of meat and scraping the bottom of the pan to remove any stuck-on bits, until the meat is browned, about 10 minutes. Use a slotted spoon to remove the beef and reserve the drippings in the skillet.

2. In the same skillet, combine the tomatoes, onion, garlic, and salt and cook over medium-high heat, stirring and scraping up any browned bits, until most of the liquid has evaporated and the tomatoes stick to the skillet, about 8 minutes.

3. Add the remaining 2 tablespoons lard, the chili powder, flour, and cumin and cook, stirring frequently, until very fragrant, about 90 seconds.

4. Add the reserved beef and toss until completely coated in the spice/flour mixture. Whisk in the broth, bring to a boil, and continue whisking, until no floury lumps remain. Reduce the heat to medium-low and simmer until the chili sauce has thickened and the beef is tender, 30 to 35 minutes. Taste and season with more salt if desired.

Do ahead: The salsa can be made up to 3 days ahead. Store in an airtight container in the refrigerator, or freeze for up to 3 months.

SWAP CORNER
Make it plant-based by subbing 1 pound chopped mushrooms for the ground beef. After adding the mushrooms to the pan, let them sit, undisturbed long enough to cook out their water and brown, 4 to 6 minutes, then remove from the pan as you would the beef.

ALSO
GREAT ON
CHILAQUILES

ENCHILADAS
GRATINADAS
PAGE 237

CRISPY CHEESY THINGS

✺ You're a mystery to me, person reading this book, but I bet you love crispy cheese. It's a beautiful, perfect thing. That's why you need Costra de Queso (page 196), a cheese-laced taco shell or shell liner, and Chicharrón de Queso (page 196) in your life. I first encountered chicharrón de queso at a restaurant in Mexico City that served this huge, sizzling roll of crispy, lacy cheese with salsa and was forever changed (*chicharrón* means "crunchy snack," and it's not always made from pork). And now you will be, too.

Use a costra de queso for any taco you're making, and serve chicharrón de queso with table salsas as you would chips/totopos.

CHICHARRÓN DE QUESO

Cheese Crackling

SERVES 4

12 ounces (340 g) medium cheddar, Monterey Jack, queso Chihuahua, or Mexican manchego cheese, grated

1. Arrange a rack in the center of the oven and preheat to 375°F. Line a sheet pan with parchment paper or a silicone baking mat (do not use foil or the cheese might stick).

2. Arrange the grated cheese in an even layer covering most of the pan. It's okay if there are some spaces between the shreds of cheese.

3. Bake until the cheese is bubbling and deep golden brown around the edges and in spots in the center, about 15 minutes.

4. Let cool for 4 minutes, then use a spatula to lift and roll the chicharrón into a large log and transfer to a large platter and let cool. Chicharrón will crisp as it sits. (If you don't feel like rolling, just let it cool and then break into chip-size shards.)

COSTRA DE QUESO

Cheese Crust

MAKES 8 CHEESE ROUNDS

6 ounces (170 g) medium cheddar, Monterey Jack, queso Chihuahua, or Mexican manchego cheese, grated

1. Arrange a rack in the center of the oven and preheat to 375°F. Line a sheet pan with parchment paper or a silicone baking mat (do not use foil or the cheese might stick).

2. Arrange the grated cheese into 8 equal rounds 3 inches wide (about 21 g each) on the prepared baking sheet and space at least 1 inch apart.

3. Bake until the cheese is bubbling and deep golden brown around the edges and in spots in the center, about 15 minutes. Let cool for 4 minutes to crisp up and place over a warm tortilla or tostada.

• Chicharrón de queso

7-

SPECIAL SALSAS

ESPE

CHAPTER

7

ESPECIAL
—SPECIAL SALSAS

There was a salsa that changed everything for me. A caramelized onion and serrano salsa I had with a torta in Mexico City (which I gushed about in the introduction to this book), and it defied all the expectations I've ever had for salsa. It was creative and delicious, simple yet unforgettable. It was a reminder that salsa can, and should, be really damn fun.

So let's have fun. These are the salsas that didn't quite fit into the categories of previous chapters. They're also some of my favorites in the book. Three versions of salsa macha, an extravagant chile con queso, and even an Alfredo-ish salsa that's great over pasta (seriously!). They're all cooked—sometimes very cooked—blended, and maybe a little mashed. The ingredients are unexpected, the methods are unorthodox, but the result is joyful and flavorful. It's time to experiment with flavors or ingredients you didn't think belonged in salsa (vanilla! ghee!) but are actually wonderful in it. We'll put together everything we've learned so far, grabbing the random stuff in our pantries, and see if it works. But because I've already tested all of these . . . we know it will.

SALSA MACHA

PEANUT SALSA MACHA
Peanuts, guajillo, and chile de árbol

Salsa macha is typically made of fried chiles ground with garlic and salt, to which fried peanuts and seeds are added. Praise be. I love it so much I have three recipes for it. One theory on the name is that macha (from macho) refers to the strength and bravery required to consume it because it's so hot, the other is that macha comes from the verb *machacar*, "to smash," because it was originally made in a molcajete. I decided to go with God and make it the traditional way, with a little Rick twist: adding piloncillo and vinegar to expand and explode the flavor, and olive oil to round things out, while also yielding more salsa.

MAKES 1½ CUPS

- 1 cup vegetable oil
- 1 cup roasted peanuts (4.8 oz/135 g)
- 6 garlic cloves, peeled and smashed (but still holding their shape)
- 3 chiles guajillos (0.8 oz/24 g), stemmed and seeded
- 10 dried chiles de árbol (0.4 oz/10 g), stemmed
- 1 chile morita (0.1 oz/2 g), stemmed
- ½ cup raw sesame seeds (1.8 oz/80 g)
- 1 tablespoon apple cider vinegar
- 1½ teaspoons Diamond Crystal kosher salt (0.21 oz/6 g), plus more to taste
- 1 teaspoon grated piloncillo (0.14 oz/4 g) or dark brown sugar
- ¼ cup extra-virgin olive oil

SERVING SUGGESTIONS

Use anywhere you'd want chile oil or chili crisp, like dumplings, roasted veggies, on pizza, soups, and stews—on anything, really.

1. In a medium saucepan, combine the oil, peanuts, and garlic and cook over medium heat until the garlic is golden brown and the peanuts are slightly deeper in color, 7 to 9 minutes (but not too dark! They burn quickly). Using a slotted spoon, transfer the garlic and peanuts to a heatproof bowl to cool.

2. Add the guajillos, chiles de árbol, and morita to the pan with the hot oil and cook over medium heat until the oil is slightly reddish and the chiles are brick red, about 30 seconds. Using a slotted spoon, transfer the chiles to the peanut mixture. Let cool for 5 minutes.

3. Remove the pan from heat and add the sesame seeds to the hot oil and set aside. They will toast as they sit.

4. Transfer the toasted chiles and garlic to a food processor and purée until coarsely ground (it should look like red pepper flakes). Add the peanuts and pulse 4 times to coarsely grind them but not make peanut butter.

5. Return to the heatproof bowl and stir in the vinegar, salt, piloncillo, and toasted sesame seeds (and the oil in the pan). Stir in the olive oil, taste, and season with more salt if desired.

Do ahead: The salsa can be made up to 2 weeks ahead. Store in an airtight container at room temperature.

SWAP CORNER
You can swap the chiles de árbol and morita for an equal amount of red pepper flakes (not chili powder!). The flavor won't be as complex, but it gets the job done in a pinch. Add them during the last minute of cooking the garlic and peanuts, and don't worry if a few flakes get left behind with the sesame seeds.

Shrimp summer rolls

Cucumber-radish
carpaccio

SALSA MACHA CON HABANEROS

SALSA MACHA WITH HABANEROS
Almonds, sesame seeds, and habanero

I went a little off the rails here, but damn, it's worth it. Fresh habaneros, lightly pickled, bring this burst of hot sweetness into the intense, toasty oil that helps temper the chiles' heat. (You can dictate the heat level by choosing how long you want to pickle them; see step 1, below.) You want to spoon this over something that needs spice, crunch, and acidity to liven things up, like deeply roasted Brussels sprouts or a summer corn salad.

MAKES 1½ CUPS

- 6 chiles habaneros (2.3 oz/66 g), stemmed, halved, and seeded
- 1½ cups distilled white vinegar
- ½ cup raw almonds (2.8 oz/80 g)
- 1 cup vegetable oil
- 2 tablespoons raw sesame seeds (0.8 oz/24 g)
- 2 garlic cloves, peeled and smashed (but still holding their shape)
- 1 teaspoon Diamond Crystal kosher salt (0.14 oz/4 g), plus more to taste

SERVING SUGGESTIONS

Spoon over eggs, fish, oysters, roasted veg like Brussels sprouts, grilled veg and skewers, grain bowls, rice bowls, brothy beans, corn salads or on the cob.

1. In a medium bowl, stir together the habaneros and vinegar. Let it sit, uncovered, for 1 to 3 hours (the chiles will lose their heat as they soak; in 1 hour, they'll have the heat level of a serrano, in 3 hours, they'll taste like a spicy poblano). Drain the chiles and discard the vinegar or save to use 1 teaspoon at a time in soups, stews, sauces, or vinaigrettes (it's killer spicy otherwise).

2. In a medium saucepan, cook the almonds and oil over medium heat until the nuts begin to smell toasted and the oil is bubbling, about 5 minutes.

3. Add the sesame seeds and garlic and remove from the heat. Let sit, uncovered, for about 10 minutes to allow the sesame seeds to toast and the oil to cool slightly.

4. Scoop out the garlic and transfer to a food processor. Add the habaneros and purée until finely chopped but not a paste. Add the salt, almonds, sesame seeds (and cooled oil from the pan) and pulse until the almonds are coarsely chopped. Taste and season with more salt if desired.

Do ahead: The salsa can be made up to 2 weeks ahead. Store in an airtight container in the refrigerator.

STORE IN THE FRIDGE, PLEASE
Because there are fresh chiles in this salsa, store it in the fridge, which may thicken the oil's consistency a little. Take it out a few minutes before using to bring it back to room temperature.

SALSA MACHA DE VAINILLA Y GHEE

Ghee, vanilla, and chilhuacle

To wrap up my salsa macha trio, I had to re-create an unforgettable one I had at Masala y Maíz, a brilliant South Asian, East African, and Mexican spot in Mexico City. This isn't the restaurant's recipe, just one based on my very fond memory of enjoying it on garam masala shrimp skewers. Yum. The hint of vanilla triggers the senses into perceiving a slight sweetness, making this so nice on shrimp. The vanilla lingers in the background and helps the other spices harmonize, opening your mind to the possibilities in your pantry.

MAKES 2 CUPS

- 1½ cups ghee or clarified butter
- ½ vanilla bean, split lengthwise, or ½ teaspoon vanilla paste
- 5 garlic cloves, peeled and smashed (but still holding their shape)
- 1 cup roasted cashews (4.6 oz/130 g)
- 10 large chiles chilhuacles amarillos (2.8 oz/78 g) or chiles guajillos, stemmed and seeded
- ½ cup chiles chiltepín (1 oz/27 g) or chiles de árbol, stemmed
- 2 tablespoons raw sesame seeds
- 1 teaspoon fennel seeds
- 1½ teaspoons Diamond Crystal kosher salt (0.2 oz/6 g), plus more to taste

SERVING SUGGESTIONS

Serve this over roasted or steamed vegetables, rice, or stir it into sour cream and mayonnaise for a crudités dip. Spoon over Fideo con Camarones (page 256) or over ice cream!

1. In a medium saucepan, combine the ghee, vanilla bean, garlic, and cashews and heat over medium until the garlic and cashews are golden brown, 5 to 7 minutes.

2. With a slotted spoon, transfer the vanilla bean, garlic, and nuts to a heatproof medium bowl to cool. When cool enough to handle, discard the vanilla pod.

3. To the same saucepan, add the chilhuacles and chiltepínes and cook over medium heat until the fat is slightly reddish and the chiles are fragrant and a deep brick red color, about 30 seconds. Using a slotted spoon, transfer the chiles to the bowl with the cashews and let cool for at least 5 minutes before puréeing.

4. Add the sesame seeds and fennel seeds to the hot pan with the ghee and remove from the heat. Let sit for about 10 minutes to allow the seeds to toast and to let the ghee cool slightly.

5. In a food processor, purée the roasted garlic until finely chopped. Add the salt, cashews, and chiles and pulse just a few times until everything is coarsely chopped. And the ghee and toasted seeds and pulse until incorporated. Taste and season with more salt if desired.

Do ahead: The salsa can be made up to 2 weeks ahead. Store in an airtight container in the refrigerator and bring to room temperature before serving.

Vanilla ice cream

Burrito

CHIPOTLES EN CREMA

CHIPOTLES IN CREAM
Chipotles in adobo, crema, and queso Chihuahua

Oops, I left the butter bubbling on the stove and it browned. But that happy accident made this creamy, tangy, smoky salsa even better. (The brown butter's nutty notes + chipotle smoke = sinful good.) Think of it as . . . queso light. I use evaporated milk, a common pantry ingredient in Mexico, because I love its concentrated milk flavor. This is unapologetically dairy-forward, and I'm so delighted with the results. The six chipotles in adobo go hard; this is not a subtle sauce. But it's comforting and complex enough to top enchiladas, chiles rellenos, or Flautas/Taquitos Ahogadas (page 260).

MAKES 1½ CUPS

- 2 tablespoons unsalted butter (1 oz/28 g)
- 6 chipotle chiles in adobo, chopped
- 1 garlic clove, finely grated
- ¾ cup evaporated milk or whole milk
- ¼ cup crema, crème fraîche, or sour cream
- 4 oz (113 g) queso Chihuahua or Monterey Jack cheese, grated

  Diamond Crystal kosher salt (optional)

1. In a medium saucepan, melt the butter over medium heat, swirling occasionally, until the milk solids have browned and smell like toasted nuts, 1 to 2 minutes.

2. Add the chipotles and garlic and cook, stirring occasionally, until the garlic begins to brown, 1 to 2 minutes.

3. Add the evaporated milk and crema, bring to a boil, and cook for 1 minute. Add the cheese, remove from the heat, and stir until completely melted. Taste and season with salt if desired.

Do ahead: The salsa can be made up to 5 days ahead. Store in an airtight container in the refrigerator.

SERVING SUGGESTIONS

El Pepito (Steak Sandwich, page 247), burritos, Chilaquiles (page 239), hard-shell tacos, tacos dorados, refried beans, Tostadas (page 113), rice, enchilada sauce, chiles rellenos, over boring steamed vegetables or plain, cooked chicken breasts. Or stir into pasta for easy mac and cheese.

MAKE IT A QUESO
Double the cheese and turn this into a chile con queso. I love you. You're welcome.

ALFREDO ROJO

RED FRED
Chiles, crema, and lard

It can't be helped. When I tried this brick red, cream salsa for the first time, I thought, *I want this on pasta with chicken.* It's sorta like a spicy Alfredo, and I'm just as surprised as you are at how that sounds. But it's delicious. The crema is cultured, which brings some fermented cheese notes that go so well with the hot red chiles, that hint of feralness from the lard, and a dash of umami in the bouillon. I didn't intend for it to be a pasta sauce, but it's a tribute to this salsa's endless versatility. It's also outrageous with roasted vegetables, albóndigas, and as a dip for pizza. I said what I said.

MAKES 2 CUPS

- 2 tablespoons rendered lard or extra-virgin olive oil
- ¼ medium white onion (3.7 oz/105 g), roughly chopped
- 3 garlic cloves, peeled and smashed (but still holding their shape)
- 1½ teaspoons Diamond Crystal kosher salt (0.21 oz/6 g), plus more to taste
- 1 large chile ancho (0.9 oz/27 g), stemmed and seeded
- 15 chiles secos/dried serranos (0.6 oz/17 g) or 10 chiles de árbol, stemmed and seeded
- ½ cup crema, crème fraîche, or sour cream
- 2 teaspoons chicken or vegetable bouillon powder (optional; see page 14)

SERVING SUGGESTIONS

Over pasta, Enchiladas (page 234), Chilaquiles (page 239), roasted veg, sandwiches, meatballs, Sonoran-Style Hot Dogs (page 275), as a dip for garlic bread or pizza. Drool.

1. In a medium saucepan, combine the lard, onion, garlic, and salt and cook over medium-high heat, stirring occasionally, until the onion and garlic are lightly browned, 6 to 8 minutes.

2. Add the anchos and chiles secos and cook, stirring occasionally, until the anchos starts to brown in spots (the spots will be lighter brown than the color of the chile, not darker brown) and the serranos are bright brick red, 60 to 90 seconds. Add 1½ cups water and bring to a boil, cover, reduce to a simmer, and cook for 5 minutes.

3. Transfer to a blender, making sure to scrape everything in, add the crema and the bouillon powder (if using), and purée until completely smooth and the thickness of heavy cream. Taste and season with more salt if desired.

Do ahead: The salsa can be made up to 5 days ahead. Store in an airtight container in the refrigerator.

Penne and grilled chicken

Fried green tomatillos

AIOLI ROJO

RED AIOLI
Morita, guajillo, garlic, and lime

I'm calling this aioli because I've worked in so many restaurant kitchens that's how I think of it. But this style of oil-emulsified salsa is common in Mexico, where obviously, they don't call it aioli, and you'll find it served alongside other salsas at your typical family carne asada. What makes it so special, as we've covered before, is that all that oil tames the chiles and captures their pure, vegetal flavors and sweetness, allowing you to use super-hot chiles you normally wouldn't eat raw. Inspired by the whole aioli thing, I added garlic, lime juice, and lime zest, so you should use it in any mayo situation.

MAKES 1½ CUPS

- 9 chiles moritas (0.8 oz/22 g), stemmed
- 2 chiles guajillos (0.6 oz/16 g), stemmed and seeded
- ½ cup vegetable oil
- 2 garlic cloves, peeled and smashed (but still holding their shape)
- 2 tablespoons fresh lime juice
- 1 teaspoon finely grated lime zest
- 1½ teaspoons Diamond Crystal kosher salt (0.21 oz/6 g), plus more to taste

SERVING SUGGESTIONS

Crab cakes (fancy!), El Pepito (Steak Sandwich, page 247), in chicken salad, potato salad, egg salad—as an all-purpose spicy mayo that reminds you what a joy it is to be alive.

1. In a medium saucepan, combine 1 cup water, the moritas, and guajillos and bring to a boil over medium-high heat. Cover, reduce to a simmer, and cook for 5 minutes. Remove from the heat and let sit for 10 minutes, until the chiles are soft and ready to blend. (Why are we boiling the chiles? See page 18.)

2. Transfer the softened chiles and ½ cup of the cooking liquid to a blender and add the oil, garlic, lime juice, lime zest, and salt and purée until smooth (it should be the consistency of aioli). Taste and season with more salt if desired.

Do ahead: The salsa can be made up to 5 days ahead. Store in an airtight container in the refrigerator.

SPICY SALMON, COMING RIGHT UP
Smother a few big spoonfuls of this aioli on a fillet of salmon and broil it (8 to 13 minutes, depending on the thickness of the fish), serving with even more aioli and a squeeze of lime on the side.

SALSA DE CEBOLLA Y SERRANO CARAMELIZADO

CARAMELIZED ONION AND SERRANO SALSA
Onion, garlic, and serrano

This salsa gets me every time. It has all the wonderful sweetness of French onion soup balanced by a heat wave of chiles serranos. It's so concentrated in flavor that a few tablespoons go a long way. I first had it slathered on a torta, but don't let that stop you from slathering it on any and all sandwiches, stirring it into your scrambled eggs, and even scooping it into stews like you would a bouillon cube. Blend it up for a spreadable salsa or use it just like the caramelized onions that they are. If you'd like to keep it on a humane heat level, use 1 to 3 serranos, and keep notes—next time, you might be ready for more.

MAKES 2 CUPS

- 6 tablespoons extra-virgin olive oil
- 4 medium white onions (3 lb/1.4 kg), sliced
- 4 garlic cloves, sliced
- 10 chiles serranos (7 oz/200 g), stemmed and sliced
- 1 tablespoon Diamond Crystal kosher salt (0.4 oz/12 g), plus more to taste

SERVING SUGGESTIONS

On burgers, Torta Milanesa (page 244), Pozole Verde con Pollo (page 271), tacos, mac and cheese. Add a spoonful with cream cheese to stuff peppers.

1. In a large pot, combine the oil, onions, garlic, serranos, and salt and cook over medium heat, stirring occasionally, until the onion is deep golden brown and very soft, 35 to 40 minutes.

2. Add ½ cup water to deglaze the pan, scraping up any browned bits from the bottom of the pan and cook until most of the water has evaporated, about 2 minutes. (Optional: Transfer to a blender and purée until spreadable but still a little chunky.) Taste and season with more salt if desired.

Do ahead: The salsa can be made up to 5 days ahead. Store in an airtight container in the refrigerator, or freeze for up to 1 month.

OH WAIT, ONE MORE
Mix a few spoonfuls of this salsa into sour cream for a spicy take on French onion dip. Outrageous.

Fried
fish taco

SALSA TÁRTARA

TARTAR SAUCE
Mayonnaise, crema, and jalapeño
en escabeche

This is a life-essential tartar SALSA. For fish tacos, forever. It begins like the salsa blanca recipe from *Mi Cocina* and then expands it with pickled jalapeños and a few other tricks from up my sleeve: a dash of Dijon, a handful of herbs. (You could also add back in the single anchovy used in *Mi Cocina*—it couldn't hurt.) And while I designed this with fried fish in mind, it's also just a great herby mayo for all of your sandwich needs, which I've heard are plentiful. Have at it.

MAKES 2 CUPS

- ¾ cup mayonnaise
- ½ cup crema, crème fraîche, or sour cream
- ¾ cup finely chopped pickled jalapeños (6.4 oz/181 g)
- ¼ medium white onion (3.7 oz/105 g), finely chopped
- 1 garlic clove, finely grated
- 1 tablespoon chopped fresh cilantro leaves with tender stems (0.14 oz/4 g)
- 1 tablespoon chopped fresh parsley leaves with tender stems (0.14 oz/4 g)
- 1 tablespoon fresh lime juice
- 1 teaspoon finely grated lime zest
- 2 teaspoons Dijon mustard, spicy hot mustard, or yellow mustard
- 1 tablespoon chopped dried chile de árbol or red pepper flakes (optional)

  Diamond Crystal kosher salt (optional)

SERVING SUGGESTIONS

All the fried seafood. All the time. Also great as a sandwich spread or mixed into chicken, egg, or tuna salad.

In a medium bowl, stir together the mayonnaise, crema, jalapeños, onion, garlic, cilantro, parsley, lime juice, lime zest, mustard, and chile de árbol (if using) until completely combined. Taste and season with salt if desired.

Do ahead: The salsa can be made up to 5 days ahead. Store in an airtight container in the refrigerator.

Bob Armstrong Chile con Queso, page 220

BOB ARMSTRONG CHILE CON QUESO

Cheese, taco meat, guacamole, and pico de gallo

This queso is the king of all quesos. It's not just queso, but a layering of spiced picadillo, *then* queso, and *then* scoops of guacamole, pico de gallo, and sour cream so that everything you could ever need in life is in one bowl. It originates from Matt's El Rancho in Austin, Texas, and is named after a former Texas land commissioner. When I was twenty-three, I moved to Dallas and went with a friend to Mattito's, a Tex-Mex spot near my house. She sat down and ordered a margarita and "a bowl of Bob." What? Who? I was so confused, until the bowl of Bob showed up and I ate the whole thing. Nothing was the same after that.

SERVES 8

PICADILLO

- 1 tablespoon vegetable oil
- 1 pound (453 g) ground beef chuck (20% fat)
- ½ medium white onion (6.5 oz/183 g), chopped
- ½ large chile poblano (3 oz/85 g), chopped
- 2 garlic cloves, finely grated
- 1½ teaspoons Diamond Crystal kosher salt (0.21 oz/6 g), plus more to taste
- ½ teaspoon freshly ground black pepper, plus more to taste
- 1½ teaspoons ground cumin
- 1 teaspoon chili powder
- 1 cup chicken stock or low-sodium chicken broth

QUESO

- 3 tablespoons unsalted butter
- ½ medium white onion (6.5 oz/183 g), chopped
- ½ large chile poblano (3 oz/85 g), chopped
- 4 chiles jalapeños (3.2 oz/91 g), stemmed and chopped
- 3 garlic cloves, finely grated
- 1½ teaspoons Diamond Crystal kosher salt (0.21 oz/6 g)
- 2 medium Roma tomatoes or tomatillos (7.8 oz/221 g), cored and chopped
- 2 tablespoons all-purpose flour (0.6 oz/16 g)
- 1½ cups whole milk, plus more if needed
- ½ pound (226 g) Monterey Jack cheese, grated
- ½ pound (226 g) medium or sharp cheddar cheese (not aged), grated

ASSEMBLY

- Pico de Gallo Clásico o Salsa Mexicana (page 62)
- Guacamole (pages 82 to 85)
- Sour cream
- Chopped fresh cilantro
- Totopos (page 112) or Tostadas (page 113), warm, for serving

1. MAKE THE PICADILLO: In a large skillet, heat the oil and beef over high and cook, breaking up the clumps with a spoon, until browned on all sides but not completely cooked through, 6 to 8 minutes. Transfer to a medium bowl, leaving behind as much fat in the pan as possible.

2. Reduce the heat to medium and add the onion, poblano, garlic, salt, and black pepper. Cook, stirring occasionally, until the vegetables are tender but not browned, 6 to 8 minutes.

3. Add the cumin and chili powder and cook, stirring, until fragrant, about 1 minute. Add the chicken stock and reserved beef along with any accumulated juices to the pan. Bring to a simmer and cook, stirring and scraping up any browned bits from the bottom of the skillet, until the liquid has evaporated, 8 to 10 minutes.

4. Taste and season with more salt and pepper if desired. Transfer to a medium bowl, cover, and let sit until ready to use.

5. MAKE THE QUESO: In a medium saucepan, melt the butter over medium heat. Add the onion, poblano, jalapeños, garlic, and salt and cook, stirring occasionally, until tender but not browned, 8 to 10 minutes.

6. Add the tomatoes and continue to cook until all the juices have evaporated and the tomatoes are beginning to fall apart, about 6 minutes.

7. Stir in the flour and cook, stirring constantly, until all of the vegetables are completely coated,

about 1 minute. Whisk in the milk and continue to whisk until the mixture comes to a boil and thickens, about 4 minutes.

8. Reduce the heat to low and gradually add both cheeses and cook, stirring constantly, until the cheese has completely melted and the queso is smooth and creamy. If it seems too thick, stir in a little more milk.

9. TO ASSEMBLE: Spread the warm picadillo in a 2-quart baking dish. Pour the hot queso over the meat mixture. Top with a generous scoop each of pico de gallo, guacamole, and sour cream. Sprinkle with cilantro and serve hot with warm totopos.

Do ahead: The picadillo and queso can be made 3 days ahead and stored separately. Cover tightly with plastic wrap and refrigerate. Reheat before assembling.

CH.7—ESPECIAL

BREAK BREAK BREAK

Good morning! Remember those commercials for cereal that always said it was "part of a complete breakfast?" Well, that turned out to be mostly lies, because the truth is that a complete breakfast requires breakfast tacos and salsa. These recipes are my favorite ways to start the day. The tacos are my everyday breakfast. I halve the recipe and have 2 or 3 tacos for breakfast, and then wrap up the leftovers for a snack or dinner later. The molletes (an open-faced bean and cheese sandwich), which are a *little* more labor intensive and filling, are my weekend brunch. You should know by now that the fillings are yours for the changing (add refried beans to your tacos or a fried egg to your mollete), but that salsa is nonnegotiable.

RICK'S BREAKFAST TACOS

Eggs and chorizo on a flour tortilla
(like Mom used to make)

SERVES 4

- 1 tablespoon extra-virgin olive oil
- 8 ounces (226 g) Mexican fresh chorizo, casings removed
- 8 large eggs
- ½ teaspoon Diamond Crystal kosher salt (0.07 oz/2 g), plus more to taste
- 8 tortillas de harina, warm
  La Mañanera (page 32), for serving

1. In a large skillet, preferably a well-seasoned cast-iron or nonstick, heat the oil over high until you see little wisps of smoke wafting up over the skillet. Add the chorizo and use a silicone spatula to break up the clumps and spread the chorizo out in an even layer across the skillet. Cook, stirring occasionally, until lightly browned or slightly darker in color from when you started, 5 to 7 minutes.

2. Meanwhile, in a large bowl, whisk the eggs and salt until no streaks of white or yolk remain.

3. When the chorizo is fully cooked, add the eggs to the skillet and reduce the heat to medium-low. Using a silicone spatula, push the eggs and chorizo around the skillet to mix them completely. Scrape across the bottom of the pan to make sure nothing is sticking and continue to cook and scrape until the eggs are fluffy and just set, about 2 minutes. Transfer to a medium bowl.

4. Divide the eggs and chorizo among the tortillas (about ⅓ cup each), top with the salsa, and have a great morning!

SWAP CORNER
You don't keep chorizo in the freezer at all times in case of emergency? Refried beans, smashed chickpeas, or sautéed peppers and onion are some swaps for you.

MOLLETES DE PANELA

SEARED PANELA OPEN-FACED SANDWICHES
Beans, seared cheese, and
pico de gallo on a roll

SERVES 4

- 5 tablespoons extra-virgin olive oil, divided
- ½ medium white onion (5.6 oz/160 g), chopped
- 2 garlic cloves, finely grated
- 2 (15-ounce) cans black beans and their liquid, or 4 cups homemade beans

  Diamond Crystal kosher salt (optional)
- 1 pound queso panela (see below) or paneer, cut into ¼-inch-thick slices

ASSEMBLY

- 4 bolillos, hoagie rolls, or another breakfast-y bread you are into
- Pico de Gallo Clásico o Salsa Mexicana (page 62)
- Sliced avocado
- Chipotles en Crema (page 209)
- Lime wedges, for squeezing

1. In a heavy medium skillet, preferably cast-iron, heat 3 tablespoons of the oil over medium. Add the onion and garlic and cook, stirring occasionally, until tender and just beginning to brown, 6 to 8 minutes.

2. Increase the heat to high. Add the beans and their liquid (the mixture will spit and sputter but will quickly settle down) and cook, stirring occasionally, until about half of the liquid has evaporated, about 5 minutes. Use a potato masher or fork to smash the beans until there are no whole beans remaining and the mixture is thick and creamy. Remove from the heat, taste and season with salt if desired. Let cool slightly; the beans will thicken as they sit.

3. In a nonstick medium skillet, heat the remaining 2 tablespoons olive oil over medium-high. Working in batches, cook the panela until seared and deep golden brown on both sides, 2 to 3 minutes per side. Transfer to a plate.

4. TO ASSEMBLE: Slice the rolls open and toast them. Spread about ⅓ cup of the beans on the bottom of each toasted roll. Top with the seared panela, avocado slices, pico de gallo, a drizzle of chipotles en crema, and a squeeze of lime.

¿QUÉ ES LA PANELA?
Panela is a firmer cheese, like paneer or Halloumi, that gets a nice sear and holds its shape. It's as satisfying as a sausage patty on a sandwich.

8-
com

EASY
MEALS

FÁCIL

8

COMIDA FÁCIL
—EASY MEALS

After making over a *million* salsas for this book, my entire perspective on it changed. Before, I'd make salsa to go *with* a dish. The salsa was a complement— it came second. But what if it came first? If you have a few different salsas in your fridge or freezer, dinner can come together so much quicker. (The secret to the freezer stash is, every time you make a salsa, put a cup or two of it in the freezer.) I've made the easiest dinners by tossing a quart of salsa in the oven with a whole chicken, and found it was always wonderful, and never the same flavor twice. I also make a lot of fried rice, tossing the salsa in the pan with rice, veg, and soy sauce and letting it cook and coat the grains. Delicious. (For a super-quick "recipe" on how to do those two and a couple more go-to salsa transformations, see page 26.)

My salsa experimenting also revealed how salsa is more than a topping, but it can be the base of a broth for tortilla soup (see Sopa de Pollo y Salsa, page 272) and a sauce to simmer meatballs in (see page 242). This chapter dives into all of the easy dinners you can make with the salsas in this book. It begins with your necessary enchiladas and chilaquiles recipes, then moves into sandwich mode, then you'll find a handful of taco fillings, followed by some hearty soups and stews, including my mom's famous Chile Colorado (see page 264), and a few happy surprises to take us home.

What Salsa Should I Use in a Dish?
I'll give you ideas in the recipes that follow. But think of what that salsa will bring to the dish, especially in a large quantity. If it's a textured pico, it could serve as chunky veg in a soup. When you're picking a salsa to marinate chicken in, you might not want a super-intense and hot fermented hot sauce.

What Salsa Should I Serve *with* a Dish?
If a dish is soft, saucy, and/or mushy (in a good way, of course), you might want a salsa to go with it that'll add some crunch, like pico de gallo or salsa macha. If you have a dish that's on the dry side, like shredded chicken tacos, look for a salsa that'll add moisture. When all else fails, go with the Chipotles en Crema (page 209), it goes with *everything*.

CH.8—COMIDA FÁCIL

ENCHILADAS, ENFRIJOLADAS, ENTOMATADAS, ENMOLADAS

Soft-toasted corn tortillas, filled and dipped in salsa

These enchiladas are Mexican-style, which means they're not baked in cheese (turn the page for that). They come together quickly, so quickly that in Mexico, they're often more of a side dish or an accompanying starch to larger mains. You warm your salsa, dip the tortilla in, fill it, fold it, and eat it. Just don't skip the prep step where you lightly toast/fry the tortilla with oil, because that's what makes it "waterproof" so it doesn't fall apart in the salsa. Fill it with yesterday's dinner leftovers, rotisserie chicken, roasted sweet potatoes, and some black beans—whatever you've got.

SERVES 4

- 12 tortillas de maíz (stale are best)
- 2 tablespoons vegetable oil
- 3 cups salsa (see Salsa Pairings, below)
- 2 cups filling, such as shredded rotisserie chicken, cooked chorizo or ground meat, roasted vegetables, or seared tofu or tempeh

  Diamond Crystal kosher salt (optional)
- 6 ounces (170 g) queso fresco, queso Cotija (crumbled), queso Oaxaca (shredded), queso Chihuahua (grated), or your favorite cheese

FOR SERVING

- Cilantro leaves with tender stems
- Chopped onion
- Crema
- Sliced avocado

SALSA PAIRINGS

Any salsa from the Enchilada/Chilaquiles section (pages 176 to 193); also great with Salsa Guajillo (page 184)—this would be the most similar to Mexican enchiladas; Los Puerquitos (page 101) for enfrijoladas; Mole Sencillo (page 178) for enmoladas.

.

1. Lightly brush both sides of each tortilla with the oil and heat a large skillet over medium-high. Working in batches, cook the tortillas until lightly browned and starting to crisp, about 1 minute per side. This will prevent the tortillas from falling apart when you fill them. Set aside until ready to assemble.

2. Pour the salsa into the same skillet and bring to a boil, then reduce the heat to low. Working with one at a time and using tongs, dip the tortillas in the salsa, wiggling and turning to completely coat, about 1 second per side. Transfer the coated tortillas to a baking sheet as you go, spaced apart and not stacked; they will soften as they sit.

3. In a medium saucepan, heat the filling over medium-low or in the microwave, until very warm but not boiling or sizzling. Taste and season with salt if desired. Spoon 2 heaping tablespoons of filling and about 1 scant tablespoon queso across the center of each tortilla; fold over like a taco. Repeat with the remaining tortillas, filling, and cheese.

4. Divide among plates and spoon the remaining warm salsa over. Top with cilantro, onion, crema, avocado, any remaining filling, and any remaining queso.

Do ahead: The only thing you can prep ahead here is the salsa. This dish is meant to be eaten immediately!

ENCHILADAS IN MEXICO

In central Mexico, enchiladas are often made with a guajillo salsa; filled with queso and onion; topped with shredded iceberg lettuce, crema, queso, and a pickled jalapeño; and served as the side for roasted chicken, potatoes, and carrots.

ENCHILADAS GRATINADAS

CHEESY BAKED ENCHILADAS
Soft-toasted corn tortillas, rolled, smothered in salsa, and baked

You're making these enchiladas because you want melted cheese. You *need* melted cheese. That's the driving force and let's not deny it. These are those Tex-Mex-style enchiladas that get nice and toasty as the cheese browns at the edges. Pure comfort. I don't often find these in Mexico (except for enchiladas suizas, which you can make using this recipe and the Salsa Suiza recipe on page 191), so when I miss home, I make them myself. If you have a salsa on hand that you're unsure would work with enchiladas, take a fork of whatever your filling would be, dip it in the salsa, and try it. Good? Then make enchiladas.

SERVES 6

- 12 tortillas de maíz (stale are best)
- 3   tablespoons vegetable oil
- 2   cups filling, such as shredded rotisserie chicken, cooked chorizo or ground meat, roasted vegetables, or seared tofu or tempeh
- 3   cups Tex-Mex Enchilada Sauce (page 192) or other salsa (see Salsa Pairings, below)

    Diamond Crystal kosher salt (optional)

- 12 ounces (340 g) queso Chihuahua, Mexican manchego, sharp cheddar, or your favorite cheese, grated

FOR SERVING

- Pico de Gallo Clásico o Salsa Mexicana (page 62)
- Guacamole of your choice (pages 82 to 85)
- Salsa de mesa (chapters 1 through 3) or Salsa Picante (pages 152 to 159)

SALSA PAIRINGS

Tex-Mex Enchilada Sauce (page 192), also great with any salsa from the Enchilada/Chilaquiles section (pages 176 to 193, Salsa Suiza (page 191, Alfredo Rojo (page 210).

1. Arrange a rack in the center of the oven and preheat to 400°F.

2. Lightly brush both sides of each tortilla with the oil and heat a large skillet over medium-high. Working in batches, cook the tortillas until lightly browned and starting to crisp, about 1 minute per side. This will prevent the tortillas from falling apart when you bake them. Set aside until ready to assemble.

3. In a medium bowl, mix the filling and ½ cup of the salsa until combined. Taste and season with salt if desired.

4. Pour ½ cup of the salsa into a 9 × 13-inch baking dish and spread to cover the bottom. Working with one at a time, arrange 2 heaping tablespoons of the filling down the center of a tortilla, roll to secure the filling, and place seam-side down in the baking dish. Repeat with the remaining tortillas and filling, making sure they're nestled right up against each other.

5. Pour the remaining salsa over the rolled tortillas, then scatter all the cheese on top.

6. Bake until the salsa is bubbling and the cheese is just beginning to brown, 15 to 20 minutes.

7. Serve warm, topped with pico de gallo, guacamole, and/or a salsa of your choice.

Do ahead: The enchiladas can be made up to 5 days ahead. Store in an airtight container in the refrigerator. Or divide any leftover enchiladas into portions of 2 or 3; wrap each portion tightly in plastic wrap or place in a freezer bag, squeeze out the air, seal, and freeze for up to 3 months.

ENCHILADA FILLING MOOD BOARD
Chorizo, beans, roasted vegetables, pulled pork, turkey, tofu.

CHILAQUILES

Totopos, salsa, and fried eggs

It's not always red or green! Chilaquiles can be made with nearly any salsa, a classic and ancient dish of tortillas chips tossed or cooked in a warm salsa. This is the dish that brings families together, because if you want roasted salsa verde on yours, and your sister wants a deep salsa roja on hers, you can make that happen since the salsa is tossed in at the end. I feel strongly that they need to be as crisp as possible, because by the end of the meal they'll get soggy and I like that journey. That's why I don't cook the chips in the salsa as many people do, but if you prefer softer chilaquiles . . . I've written that variation below.

SERVES 4

- 2 tablespoons vegetable oil
- 4 large eggs
  - Diamond Crystal kosher salt
- 3 cups salsa (see Salsa Pairings, below)
  - Totopos (page 112) or 1 (10-ounce) bag corn chips
- 2 cups protein (optional), such as shredded rotisserie chicken, cooked chorizo or ground meat, roasted vegetables, or seared tofu or tempeh, warm

FOR SERVING

- Sliced red onion
- Chopped fresh cilantro
- Cut avocado
- Crumbled queso fresco
- Crema

SALSA PAIRINGS

Any salsa from the Enchilada/Chilaquiles section (pages 176 to 193); also great with La Manteca (page 105), La Pasilla (page 106), Salsa Costeño (page 188).

1. In a large nonstick skillet, heat the oil over medium-high. Crack the eggs into the skillet, leaving space around each one, and cook until the whites are set and the edges are crisp, about 4 minutes. Season with salt and transfer to a plate.

2. In the same skillet, bring the salsa to a boil over medium-high heat.

> **For softer chilaquiles,** add the totopos to the hot salsa and cook, tossing to completely coat, until very hot.

> **For crispy chilaquiles,** add the totopos to a large bowl and pour over about three-quarters of the hot salsa and toss until completely coated.

3. Immediately—no dilly-dallying!—serve the chilaquiles on a plate topped with your favorite protein (if using), a fried egg, red onion, cilantro, avocado, queso fresco, and crema. For the crispy chilaquiles, top with the remaining salsa drizzled over.

Albóndingas Sub, page 242

ALBÓNDIGAS SUB

Meatballs and salsa on a roll

I never met a meatball I didn't love. (Put that on my headstone, please.) I also love almost anything served between two buns. Albóndigas (Mexican meatballs) are so easy to make and so forgiving (you can even smash the meat into a loaf pan for meatloaf). You could add a tablespoon of fermented hot sauce to the meat mixture, or a strong dried chile salsa like La Pasilla (page 106) or La Morita (page 102). For the salsa that they cook in, however, you want to go with something more balanced and watery since it'll cook down with the meatballs and become the dominant flavor on the sub.

SERVES 4

ALBÓNDIGAS

- 1 cup panko bread crumbs, fresh bread crumbs, or crushed Totopos (page 112)
- ⅓ cup finely chopped fresh cilantro (1.7 oz/50 g), plus more for serving
- ¼ large white onion (3.6 oz/101 g), grated on the large holes of a box grater
- 1 to 3 tablespoons Salsa Picante (optional; page 152 to 159)
- 3 garlic cloves, finely grated
- 2¼ teaspoons Diamond Crystal kosher salt (0.31 oz/9 g), plus more to taste
- 1 teaspoon freshly ground black pepper
- ¾ teaspoon cumin seeds or ½ teaspoon ground cumin
- ½ cup crema or sour cream
- 1 egg, beaten to blend
- 2 pounds (907 g) ground beef (20% fat)
- 2 tablespoons extra-virgin olive oil, plus more for shaping
- 3 cups salsa (see Salsa Pairings)

ASSEMBLY

- 1 large, soft loaf French bread or 4 bolillos or hoagie rolls, split horizontally and toasted
- Bob Armstrong Chile con Queso (page 220), guacamole of choice (pages 82 to 85), or crema, for serving
- Queso fresco or your favorite cheese, for serving

SALSA PAIRINGS

Any salsa from the Enchilada/Chilaquiles section (pages 176 to 193), also great with La Mañanera (page 32), La Molcajeteada (page 35), La Tatemada Cremosa (page 36).

1. **MAKE THE ALBÓNDIGAS:** In a large bowl, whisk together the panko, cilantro, onion, salsa (if using), the garlic, salt, pepper, and cumin until combined. Stir in the crema and egg. Add the beef and use two forks to begin "pulling" the ground beef apart as if you were shredding pulled pork, breaking up the clumps without compacting the meat into a dense mass. Continue to pull the meat apart until thoroughly mixed, no clumps of beef remain, and all the ingredients are evenly incorporated.

2. Lightly oil your hands. Scoop out portions of the meat mixture with a ¼-cup measuring cup or 2-ounce (#20) cookie scoop. Roll the meat mixture gently between your hands into balls and arrange them on a sheet pan.

3. In a large nonstick skillet over medium-high, heat the oil. Add half of the meatballs and cook, using tongs or a fork to turn and roll them occasionally, until browned on all sides, about 5 minutes. They will not be cooked through, just browned on the outside. Return the meatballs to the sheet pan and repeat with the remaining uncooked meatballs.

4. Return all the meatballs to the skillet with any accumulated juices and add the salsa and 1 cup water. Reduce the heat to medium-low, cover, and simmer until the meatballs are cooked through, 30 to 40 minutes. Taste and season with more salt if desired.

5. **TO ASSEMBLE:** Arrange the albóndigas on the bottom half of the bread. Top with the skillet salsa, drizzle with chile con queso and top with queso fresco. Top with the other half of the bread, cut into sandwiches, if desired, and serve.

Do ahead: The albóndigas can be made up to 5 days ahead. Store in an airtight container in the refrigerator.

CREMA IN MEATBALLS?
This is my secret for making them extra juicy and tender, especially if your beef is on the leaner side, or if you're making this recipe with turkey or ground chicken (which you can!).

TORTA MILANESA

Fried chicken cutlets, salsa, and cheese on a roll

This is one of Mexico's most famous tortas, and what's not to love? Breaded chicken between bread with avocado, a smear of beans, herbs, and onion, and some chewy cheese. Everybody wins. I also like to make it with eggplant, pressed tofu, zucchini, beef, pork, or panela/paneer—it's all about the cooking method, really, so use the recipe below as your template and make sure your slices are thin. The bean salsa—Los Puerquitos (page 101)—is amazing as a schmear, and then you can top with your favorite hot sauce or salsa to bring the heat.

SERVES 4

- 4 boneless, skinless chicken breasts (6 oz/170 g each)

  Diamond Crystal kosher salt and freshly ground black pepper

- ¾ cup all-purpose flour

- 3 large eggs, at room temperature

- 3 cups panko bread crumbs or dried plain bread crumbs

- ½ cup vegetable oil

- 2 cups guacamole of choice (pages 82 to 85) or 2 large avocados, peeled, seeded, and halved

- 4 bolillos or hoagie rolls, split horizontally and toasted

- 2 cups Los Puerquitos (page 101) or bacon-y refried beans (see page 250)

- ½ medium white onion (5.6 oz/160 g), thinly sliced

- 1 cup packed pápalo, an anise-like Mexican herb (1 oz/30 g) or a combination of cilantro, basil, and mint (or shredded lettuce will work, too)

- 8 ounces (226 g) queso Oaxaca or fresh mozzarella cheese, pulled into thin strands or shredded

  Chiles Encurtidos (page 149) or sliced pickled jalapeños, plus brine from the jar

1. Place a chicken breast between two sheets of plastic wrap and pound to a ¼-inch thickness. Unwrap and set aside on a plate. Repeat with the remaining breasts, then season both sides with salt and pepper.

2. Set up a dredging station in three shallow bowls or pie plates: Add the flour to one bowl. Beat the eggs in a second bowl to combine. Place the panko in the third. Season all three bowls with salt and pepper.

3. Working with one chicken cutlet at a time, dredge in the flour, shaking off any excess and making sure both sides are well coated. Transfer to the bowl with the eggs and turn to coat. Lift from the eggs, letting any excess drip off. Add the cutlet to the panko, pressing it into the crumbs on both sides to adhere, then transfer to a sheet pan. Repeat with the remaining cutlets.

4. Line a large plate with paper towels and have near the stove. In a large skillet, heat ¼ cup of the oil over medium-high. Add 2 cutlets at a time, without overlapping, and cook until the coating is deep golden brown and the chicken is just cooked through, about 3 minutes per side. Transfer to the paper towels. Wipe out the skillet and repeat with the remaining ¼ cup oil and 2 cutlets.

5. Spread some of the guacamole on the top half of each toasted bolillo. Spread some Los Puerquitos on the bottom half and set a chicken milanesa over. Top each cutlet with the onion, pápalo, queso, Chiles Encurtidos, and a generous drizzle of the brine. Place the lid on top, cut in half, and serve.

No do-ahead! Make it and eat it!

SALSA PAIRINGS

Any salsa you love, to be honest.

EL PEPITO

STEAK SANDWICH
Steak and guacamole on a roll

During my early years in New York, I had this torta for the first time in the East Village and I distinctly remember thinking: Guacamole on steak? I was a different person after that. This steak torta is one of my favorites, but honestly you could just make the marinated steak part—and serve with guacamole, of course—and be sublimely happy.

MAKES 4 TORTAS

MARINATED STEAK

- 3 tablespoons fresh lime juice
- 3 tablespoons extra-virgin olive oil
- 3 garlic cloves, finely grated, divided
- 1½ teaspoons Diamond Crystal kosher salt (0.21 oz/6 g)
- 1½ pounds (680 g) flank or skirt steak, cut to fit your skillet

TORTA

- 4 large scallions, root ends trimmed
- 1 tablespoon extra-virgin olive oil
- Chipotles en Crema (page 209), Aioli Rojo (page 213), or mayonnaise, for serving
- 4 bolillos or hoagie rolls, split horizontally and toasted
- 1 cup guacamole of choice (pages 82 to 85) or 2 ripe avocados, peeled, seeded, and sliced
- 4 to 8 Chiles Encurtidos (page 149) or sliced pickled jalapeños, quartered lengthwise
- 1 packed cup fresh cilantro leaves and tender stems (2.3 oz/64 g)
- 2 medium Roma tomatoes (9.2 oz/261 g), sliced

1. MARINATE THE STEAK: In a medium bowl, mix together the lime juice, oil, garlic, and salt until completely combined. Toss the steak in the marinade to coat and let it sit until ready to cook, for at least 30 minutes, unrefrigerated, or cover tightly with plastic wrap and refrigerate for up to 6 hours.

2. MAKE THE TORTA: Heat a large skillet, preferably cast-iron, over high until very hot, about 2 minutes. (Alternatively, use the grill.) Add the scallions and cook until charred all over, 3 to 5 minutes. Transfer to a plate and set aside until ready to serve.

3. Add the oil to the hot skillet and cook the steaks (they will soak up all of the marinade so no need to drain them), until charred on both sides, 2 to 3 minutes per side for medium-rare. Let rest for 10 minutes before slicing. Slice, against the grain, into thin strips.

4. Spread a generous amount of chipotles en crema on both sides of each bolillo and divide the steak among the 4 bottoms. Top each with the guacamole, chiles encurtidos, cilantro, and tomatoes. Serve with the charred scallion.

SWAP CORNER
Swap the steak for 1½ pounds sliced mushrooms. Marinate and brown them just as you would the steak.

CHICHARRONES EN SALSA

PORK RINDS IN SALSA
Chicharrones and salsa in a taco or as a breakfast main

There's a version of this dish in *Mi Cocina,* but if you already have salsa in the fridge or freezer it comes together so. much. faster. It's a classic stew of fried pork rinds (see Chicharrones, page 15) softened in salsa. They get very tender but not mushy, and you end up with this saucy pork filling that's great in tacos or on a platter with rice and beans, or pour it over chilaquiles for some texture contrast to the crispy chips—or cut to the chase and just eat it all with a bag of totopos. I love a salsa verde like the one on page 183 here, or tomato-based salsa that's liquidy enough to cook down a little.

SERVES 4 TO 6

- 2 tablespoons rendered lard or vegetable oil
- 12 ounces (340 g) chicharrones, broken into bite-size pieces (about 4 cups)
- 2 cups salsa (see Salsa Pairings, below)

  Diamond Crystal kosher salt (optional)

FOR SERVING

- Tortillas de maíz
- Refried beans
- Queso fresco

SALSA PAIRINGS

La Manteca (page 105), for extra porkiness; Salsa "BBQ" de Albaricoque y Chipotle (page 129), Salsa de Jamaica (page 133), Salsa Verde Tatemada (page 183).

1. In a large skillet, preferably cast-iron, heat the lard over medium-high. Add the chicharrones and cook, tossing occasionally, until browned in spots, 4 to 6 minutes.

2. Carefully add the salsa (it will spit and sputter, so stand back) and cook, stirring constantly until the bubbling has settled down, about 60 seconds. Add 1 cup water and bring to a boil. Reduce to a simmer and cook, uncovered and stirring occasionally, until the chicharrones are soft and tender and most of the liquid has evaporated, about 8 minutes. Taste and season with salt if desired.

Do ahead: The dish can be made up to 2 days ahead. Store in an airtight container in the refrigerator.

TOSTADAS DE TINGA DE POLLO

Shredded chicken and salsa on a tostada

By now you may have realized that rotisserie chicken is my secret weapon. When I'm busy and facing a fridge full of salsa, it's the answer. One of my favorite ways to use it is just to pull the meat and warm it in salsa to make a quick tinga. A typical tinga has a guajillo salsa (see page 184), but don't let that limit you. A salsa verde, or any chipotle salsa, would be wonderful, and even the tomato/avocado salsa (Aguacate Ahumado, page 77), which will create a rich, creamy sauce for the shredded chicken. The recipe also includes homemade bacon-y refried beans for a comforting contrast.

SERVES 4

- 4 ounces (113 g) smoked bacon, sliced into thin strips
- ½ medium white onion (7 oz/198 g), chopped
- 2 (15-ounce) cans black beans, undrained
- 1 chipotle chile in adobo, chopped
- 2 tablespoons adobo sauce

  Diamond Crystal kosher salt (optional)
- 2 cups cooked shredded chicken (from a roast chicken or rotisserie chicken)
- 1½ cups Salsa Guajillo (page 184) or other salsa (see Salsa Pairings, below)
- 8 Tostadas (page 113)
- 4 ounces (113 g) queso fresco, crumbled

FOR SERVING

- Cilantro leaves and tender stems, for serving
- Chopped white onion, for serving

SALSA PAIRINGS

La Pasilla (page 106), Aguacate Ahumado (page 77), Salsa al Pastor (page 174), Salsa Guajillo (page 184).

1. Place the bacon in a large (room-temperature) skillet, preferably cast-iron, and heat over medium-high. (We are starting in a cold skillet so that the bacon fat starts to melt as the pan heats and won't stick.) Cook, stirring occasionally, until the bacon is browned and crispy, about 6 minutes. Transfer to a small heatproof bowl.

2. Add the onion to the bacon fat in the skillet and cook over medium-high heat, tossing occasionally, until tender and brown, about 6 minutes.

3. Add the black beans and their liquid (that's right—don't drain them!), the bacon, chipotle, and adobo sauce and bring to a boil. Cook, stirring occasionally, until the liquid has reduced slightly, about 5 minutes.

4. Using a potato masher, smash the beans until almost no whole beans remain and the mixture is thick, smooth, and creamy—the consistency of sour cream. Remove from the heat, taste, and season with salt if desired. The refried beans will thicken as they sit.

5. In a medium saucepan over medium high, heat the chicken and salsa guajillo, stirring occasionally, until the chicken is completely coated and warmed through. Taste and season with salt if desired.

6. Spread about ⅓ cup of the refried beans over each tostada. Top with about ½ cup of the chicken tinga, the queso fresco, cilantro, and chopped onion.

Do ahead: The tinga can be made up to 5 days ahead. Store in an airtight container in the refrigerator.

PICADILLO DE RES CON PAPAS

GROUND BEEF AND POTATOES
Beef, poblano, tomato, and potato

This reminds me of my mom's cooking so much that it's what I make when I've had a rough day (or week, or month, or year) and need comfort. Every Mexican American household has their own version of picadillo, a spiced sauté of ground meat with any number of additions, from potatoes to raisins. Ours was called "stuff." It was stew-y and bulked up with potatoes; you can serve it as a main course stew with tortillas and salsa, or use in tacos, tostadas, or as a filling for enchiladas.

SERVES 4

- 2 tablespoons extra-virgin olive oil, divided
- 1 pound (453 g) ground beef (20% fat)
- ½ medium white onion (7 oz/198 g), chopped
- 2 medium Roma tomatoes (7.2 oz/204 g), cored and chopped
- 1 large chile poblano (6 oz/170 g), stemmed, seeded, and chopped
- 3 garlic cloves, finely grated
- 1 teaspoon ground cumin
- ½ teaspoon freshly ground black pepper
- 1 tablespoon Diamond Crystal kosher salt (0.4 oz/12 g), plus more to taste
- 1 medium Yukon Gold potato (7.8 oz/220 g), chopped
- 2 cups chicken stock or low-sodium chicken broth
- ¼ cup chopped fresh cilantro leaves with tender stems (0.6 oz/16 g)

FOR SERVING

- Tortillas

SALSA PAIRINGS

Guacamole con Tomatillos (page 84), Mom's Salsa de Mesa (page 54), Aguacate Ahumado (page 77), and Pico de Gallo Clásico o Salsa Mexicana (page 62).

1. In a large skillet, heat 1 tablespoon of the oil over high. Add the beef and cook, breaking up any clumps with a wooden spoon, until browned but not completely cooked through, about 5 minutes. Transfer to a medium bowl.

2. Reduce the heat to medium and add the remaining 1 tablespoon oil to the skillet. Add the onion, tomatoes, poblano, garlic, cumin, black pepper, and salt and cook, stirring occasionally, until tender but not browned, about 5 minutes.

3. Return the beef along with any accumulated juices to the pan and add the potato and stock. Bring to a simmer and cook, stirring and scraping up browned bits, until the potato is tender, 20 to 25 minutes. Taste and season with more salt if desired.

4. Mix in the cilantro just before serving. Serve with tortillas and salsa.

Do ahead: The picadillo can be made up to 3 days ahead. Store in an airtight container in the refrigerator, or freeze for up to 3 months.

MAKE IT A TACO
My dad would smash and reheat the leftovers for breakfast tacos the next morning—one of the best things about going back home for the weekend. But if you want more of a ground beef/taco night picadillo without the potatoes, turn to page 220 for the version in the Bob Armstrong Chile con Queso.

PICADILLO DE CHORIZO Y CAMARONES

Chorizo, shrimp, and jalapeño

Picadillo just means "hash"—anything chopped or mixed up. What happens when you mix up chorizo and shrimp? I about die of happiness. These two very different things were made to be together. The deep, warm spices from the chorizo coat the shrimp and you have this spicy yet sweet textured taco filling. A little spoonful of a fermented hot sauce like the four-day fermented jalapeño sauce on page 152 makes everything explode with flavor. Use this in tacos, tostadas, or enchiladas, or just enjoy it as a main course.

SERVES 4

- 3 tablespoons extra-virgin olive oil, divided
- 1 pound (453 g) Mexican fresh chorizo
- 1 pound (453 g) extra-large shrimp, peeled and deveined
- 4 large Roma tomatoes (12 oz/340 g), cored and chopped
- ½ medium white onion (6 oz/170 g), chopped
- 3 medium chiles jalapeños (5 oz/141 g), stemmed and chopped
- 4 garlic cloves, finely grated
- 2 teaspoons Diamond Crystal kosher salt (0.28 oz/8 g), plus more to taste
- 1 teaspoon ground coriander
- 1 teaspoon dried oregano, preferably Mexican
- ¼ cup chopped fresh cilantro leaves with tender stems (0.56 oz/16 g)
- Salsa (see Salsa Pairings, below), for serving

SALSA PAIRINGS

Guacamole de la Playa (page 85),
Salsa Picante de Jalapeño (page 152),
Xnipec (page 66).

1. In a large skillet, heat 1 tablespoon of the oil over high. Add the chorizo and cook, breaking up any clumps with a wooden spoon, until browned but not completely cooked through, about 5 minutes. Transfer to a medium bowl.

2. Add 1 tablespoon of the oil to the skillet, add half of the shrimp, and cook until lightly browned and just cooked through, about 1 minute per side. Transfer to plate and repeat with the remaining 1 tablespoon oil and shrimp.

3. Reduce the heat under the skillet to medium-high and add the tomatoes, onion, jalapeños, garlic, salt, coriander, and oregano and cook, stirring occasionally, until tender and the tomatoes are falling apart, 8 to 10 minutes.

4. Return the chorizo along with any accumulated juices to the pan and add 1 cup water. Bring to a simmer and cook, stirring and scraping up browned bits, until the chorizo is tender, 20 to 25 minutes.

5. Stir in the shrimp and any accumulated juices and cook until just heated through. Mix in the cilantro just before serving and top with salsa.

Do ahead: The picadillo can be made up to 3 days ahead. Store in an airtight container in the refrigerator, or freeze for up to 3 months.

FIDEO CON CAMARONES

Shrimp, vermicelli, and tomatillo

You rarely see fideo and shrimp together, so I decided to make my own destiny. The life-changing detail is to quickly toast the fideo noodles in the pan, which transforms them from tasting like nothing to tasting like nutty, toasted grain. Then, when you cook it in the salsa, the liquid will soak into the fideo and flavor them further, while the shrimp cooks to bouncy perfection. Salsa macha is my favorite condiment for soups, stews, and fideo: It adds heat and crunch from the chopped nuts that an otherwise soft dish is crying out for.

SERVES 4

- 8 ounces (226 g) fideo, vermicelli, or angel hair pasta, broken into 2-inch pieces
- 2 tablespoons rendered lard, bacon fat, or extra-virgin olive oil
- 1 pound (453 g) extra-large shrimp, peeled and deveined
- 4 medium tomatillos (8.4 oz/240 g), husked, rinsed, and thinly sliced
- ½ medium white onion (7 oz/198 g), chopped
- 1 large chile poblano (6 oz/170 g), stemmed, seeded, and chopped
- 3 chiles serranos (2 oz/57 g), stemmed and thinly sliced
- 2 garlic cloves, thinly sliced
- 4 teaspoons Diamond Crystal kosher salt (0.6 oz/16 g), plus more to taste
- 2½ cups low-sodium shrimp stock, fish stock, clam juice, or water

FOR SERVING

- 1 large avocado, peeled, seeded, and sliced
- ¼ cup fresh cilantro leaves with tender stems (0.6 oz/16 g)
- Salsa Macha de Vainilla y Ghee (page 206)

SALSA PAIRINGS

El Pepino (page 98), Serrano Frito (page 90).

1. Heat a large dry skillet over high for 2 minutes. Add the fideo and cook, tossing constantly, until most of the fideo is browned and toasted, 3 to 4 minutes. Transfer to a heatproof medium bowl and set aside until ready to use.

2. Heat 1 tablespoon of the lard in the same skillet over high. Add half of the shrimp and cook until cooked through and just beginning to brown, about 1 minute per side. Transfer to a plate. Repeat with the remaining 1 tablespoon lard and shrimp.

3. Reduce the heat under the skillet to medium-high. Add the tomatillos, onion, poblano, serranos, garlic, and salt and cook, tossing occasionally, until tender and just beginning to brown, 6 to 8 minutes.

4. Add the stock and reserved fideo and bring to a boil. Cover, reduce the heat to medium-low, and simmer until all of the liquid has been absorbed, 17 to 22 minutes. (The time range is wide because of the type of pasta you may be using and if you are using fresh or frozen shrimp.) Remove from the heat and let sit for 5 minutes.

5. Arrange the shrimp on top, cover, and let sit for 5 minutes to heat the shrimp through.

6. Serve the fideo topped with the avocado slices and cilantro leaves and top with salsa.

SWAP CORNER

Instead of shrimp, you could sear and use your favorite chicken cut, tofu, a can of chickpeas, or sauté a pile of greens. Just pick something relatively quick-cooking.

COMIDA FÁCIL

PUFFY TACOS

Fried corn tortillas, filling, and salsa

Puffy tacos are a San Antonio thing, and they're exactly what they sound like. Puffed up, fried corn tortilla shells that are shatteringly crisp. They're so much fun just to look at, though when I see them now, they remind me of lips plumped with too much filler. I still want to eat them, however, at every opportunity. The reason the tortillas puff up is because they're fresh, and so there's moisture in them that steams and expands in the frying oil. If you have older tortillas, they won't puff up the same, but all's not lost—you'll still have a crispy, toasted corn tortillas that are bendable and can be folded into a taco.

MAKES 8 TACOS

Vegetable oil, for frying

8 tortillas de maíz

FOR SERVING

- 2 cups taco filling (see Taco Fillings, below)
- Shredded iceberg lettuce
- Chopped tomatoes
- Grated sharp cheddar cheese
- Pico de Gallo Clásico o Salsa Mexicana (page 62)
- Your favorite salsa
- Chopped fresh cilantro
- Lime wedges, for squeezing

Optional equipment:
A deep-fry thermometer

TACO FILLINGS

Tinga de Pollo (see page 250), Picadillo de Res con Papas (page 252), Picadillo de Chorizo y Camarones (page 255), Chicharrones en Salsa (page 249).

1. Line a baking sheet with paper towels and have near the stove. Pour 3 inches of oil into a large heavy saucepan and fit with a deep-fry thermometer, if using. Heat over high until the thermometer registers 375°F or until the edge of a tortilla dipped into the oil bubbles vigorously.

2. Use tongs to hold one tortilla at a time perpendicular to the oil near the edge of the pot, then carefully drop it into the oil so that the tortilla slides all the way to the bottom like a diver in a pool (this method will fry and seal both sides of the tortilla, allowing steam to inflate—or "puff"—the tortilla like a balloon).

3. After a few seconds, the puffy tortilla will float to the surface. Use tongs to turn it over and with a metal spatula (like a fish spatula) in the other hand, push the top edge into the center of the tortilla, so that it folds into a taco shell shape, then continue to push it below the oil's surface. Hold in place and cook until the indentation is set and the shell is golden brown and crisp, about 1 minute. Invert the taco shell onto the paper towels to drain. Repeat with the remaining tortillas.

4. Spoon the filling into the shells and top with lettuce, tomatoes, cheddar, pico de gallo, salsa, and chopped cilantro. Serve with lime wedges for squeezing.

No do-ahead! Serve and eat immediately!

FLAUTAS OR TAQUITOS AHOGADAS

Crispy rolled tortillas filled and drowned or dipped in salsa

In Mexico, we call these flautas—because they look like long (10 inches or more) fried flutes—and in the US, people call them taquitos (and they're more like 6 inches). Either way, a filled, rolled, and fried taco can't steer you wrong, and they're easier to make at home than you think, because a toothpick helps keep the flute shape. Get creative filling it with whatever you want—mashed potatoes and cheese, poblanos and corn—just serve your rolled, fried thing in (yes, *in,* not just with!) a bowl of salsa for constant dipping.

SERVES 4 TO 6

4 cups shredded cooked chicken (from a roast chicken or rotisserie chicken)

Diamond Crystal kosher salt and freshly ground black pepper

16 tortillas de maíz

Vegetable oil, for deep-frying

4 cups salsa (see Salsa Pairings, below)

FOR SERVING

- Crema
- Crumbled queso Cotija
- Chopped fresh cilantro
- Shredded iceberg lettuce
- Chopped white onion
- Lime wedges; for squeezing

Optional equipment:
A deep-fry thermometer

SALSA PAIRINGS, FOR DROWNING

Any salsa from the Enchilada/Chilaquiles section (pages 176 to 193).

SALSA PAIRINGS, FOR DIPPING

Bob Armstrong Chile con Queso (page 220), La Mañanera (page 32).

1. In a medium bowl, generously season the chicken with salt and pepper and toss to combine. Spoon 2 to 3 tablespoons of the shredded chicken across the center of a tortilla. Fold one side over the filling, then tightly roll up the tortilla and secure it with a toothpick. Repeat with the remaining chicken and tortillas.

2. Line a sheet pan with paper towels and have near the stove. Pour ¾ inch of oil into a large heavy skillet, preferably cast-iron, and heat on high until the temperature reaches 350°F or until the edge of a tortilla dipped into the oil bubbles vigorously.

3. Working in batches, fry the flautas/taquitos, turning occasionally, until all sides are deep golden brown, 3 to 4 minutes. Transfer to the paper towels. Continue frying the remaining flautas/taquitos.

4. Divide the salsa among large soup bowls and arrange 4 flautas/taquitos on the rim of the bowl so that one end is drowning in the salsa. Top with crema, Cotija, cilantro, lettuce, onion, and a squeeze of lime.

No do-ahead! Serve and eat immediately!

QUESADILLAS LAS MEJORES

TRULY THE BEST QUESADILLAS
Toasted tortillas, melted cheese, and seared mushrooms

You might think you don't need a quesadilla recipe and I'm happy for you, but . . . I have this technique, and it makes the best quesadilla you've ever had in your life. When the pan is hot and ready for action, drop your tortilla in and toast it for a minute, then flip it and add your fillings. That's it. One tiny extra step. The toasting helps bring out the tortilla's toasted corn flavor while insulating your fillings, aka, keeping your quesadilla from a soggy, sad death. This is an especially crucial technique with meh grocery store tortillas because it begins to cook off those weird preservative flavors.

SERVES 4

- 4 tablespoons extra-virgin olive oil, divided
- 8 ounces (226 g) cremini mushrooms, cleaned and quartered
-   Diamond Crystal kosher salt
- 2 medium chiles poblanos (9.5 oz/268 g), stemmed, seeded, and cut into strips
- ½ medium white onion (7 oz/201 g), roughly chopped
- 3 garlic cloves, chopped
- 8 ounces (226 g) queso Chihuahua or your favorite melting cheese, grated
- 16 tortillas de maíz or harina de trigo
-   Salsa (see Salsa Pairings, below), for serving

SALSA PAIRINGS

Any salsa your heart desires, but especially La Borracha (page 51).

1. In a large heavy skillet, preferably cast-iron, heat 2 tablespoons of the oil over medium-high until you see wisps of smoke wafting over the skillet. Add the mushrooms and spread them out evenly across the skillet and let sit without moving them for about 2 minutes, or until golden brown. They will sear and caramelize and develop amazing flavor.

2. Now toss so that most of the mushrooms are seared-side up. You don't have to manually flip each one, just try to get a majority. Let sit for another 2 minutes undisturbed. Toss and season liberally with salt. Transfer to a bowl and set aside.

3. Add the remaining 2 tablespoons oil to the skillet and heat over medium-high. Add the poblanos, onion, garlic, and 1 teaspoon salt (0.14 oz/4 g) and cook, stirring occasionally, until the onion is tender and is just starting to brown, 6 to 8 minutes. Transfer to the bowl with the mushrooms and toss to combine. Taste and season with more salt if desired.

4. Use a paper towel to wipe the skillet clean and reheat it over medium-high (or heat a large griddle or comal).

5. Place one or more tortillas in the hot skillet or griddle and toast until browned in spots but not crispy on one side, 1 to 2 minutes. Flip the tortilla and scatter 2 tablespoons of the cheese over one half of the toasted side. Top the cheese with 2 tablespoons of the mushroom/onion mixture and fold the tortilla in half. Flatten the quesadilla by pressing down with a spatula to seal both sides with the melted cheese. Continue cooking, turning once or twice and pressing occasionally, until the cheese is melted and the tortilla begins to brown and crisp in spots (adjust the heat if needed), about 3 minutes. Transfer the quesadilla to a plate. Repeat with the remaining tortillas, cheese, and mushroom/onion mixture.

6. Serve warm with salsa.

No do-ahead! Serve and eat immediately!

GLORIA'S CHILE COLORADO

Pork stewed in dried chiles

Chile *colorado* means chile that is "colored red" (not from the state of Colorado), and my mom always used dried chiles to make a spice mix rather than a container of chili powder. The dried chiles create a deeper, more complex flavor, not to mention that bright red color and glossy, velvety texture. It takes some time to prepare (hey, not as much as mole!), but the techniques used aren't difficult. Make it when the weather's cold. Make it when you're sad, happy, or grouchy. Make it when you want to feel completely, utterly, at home.

SERVES 8

- 5 large chiles anchos (3.2 oz/92 g), stemmed and seeded
- 2 large chiles pasillas (1 oz/28 g), stemmed and seeded
- 2 large chiles guajillos (0.9 oz/25 g), stemmed and seeded
- 6 garlic cloves, chopped
- 2 bay leaves, fresh or dried
- 2 teaspoons chopped fresh sage or 1 teaspoon dried
- 1 teaspoon cumin seeds
- 1 teaspoon dried oregano, preferably Mexican
- 2 tablespoons plus 1 teaspoon Diamond Crystal kosher salt (1 oz/28 g), plus more to taste
- 1 teaspoon freshly ground black pepper
- 2 tablespoons rendered lard or vegetable oil
- 2 pounds (907 g) boneless pork shoulder into ½-inch pieces

SERVING SUGGESTIONS

This is great to make tacos or enchiladas with flour or corn tortillas, or serve it with rice and beans for a complete meal.

1. In a large saucepan, combine 3 cups water, the anchos, pasillas, guajillos, garlic, bay leaves, sage, cumin seeds, oregano, salt, and pepper and bring to a boil over high heat. Cover, remove from the heat, and let sit until the chiles are very soft and tear easily, about 15 minutes. (Why are we boiling the chiles? See page 18.)

2. Transfer the chile mixture and all the liquid to a blender and purée until very smooth.

3. Meanwhile, in a large heavy pot or Dutch oven, heat the lard over medium-high. Working in batches, cook the pork, stirring occasionally, until lightly golden brown on a few sides, 8 to 10 minutes. Transfer to a bowl and continue with the remaining pork.

4. Pour the chile purée into the pot with the pork and transfer the pork and any accumulated juices from the bowl to the pot and bring to a boil. Cover, reduce to a simmer, and cook, stirring occasionally, until the pork is very tender, can be pulled apart easily, and the salsa is a thick and mahogany-red color, about 2 hours. Taste and season with more salt if desired.

Do ahead: The chile can be made up to 3 days ahead. Store in an airtight container in the refrigerator, or freeze for up to 3 months.

WHERE'S THE SALSA?
You know what? You don't need any salsa with this. I just really wanted it in this book.

MOM'S ROLLING PIN

When I was coming home on weekends during college at the University of Texas, my mom would ask me what I wanted her to cook, and I always asked for this brick-red chile colorado, because I knew she'd make homemade flour tortillas to go with it, too. I'd open the front door and get hit with this intense smell of cumin, sage, chiles, and oregano plucked from our garden. Then I'd hear the rolling pin click-click-clicking on the granite countertop and feel completely, utterly, at home. It's one of my favorite food memories. Now, I have her rolling pin.

COSTILLAS EN CHILE VERDE

PORK RIBS IN GREEN CHILE
Pork ribs, poblano, and tomatillo

When I had this dish for the first time, I was at my uncle Eddie's house in California, and he was simmering pork neck bones in a chile verde. I tasted it, and suddenly I could see the world in color like in *The Wizard of Oz* (the chile verde is my Emerald City). The acidic and spicy poblano/tomatillo sauce cuts through the fatty pork ribs in heavenly balance. It's comforting and filling, and gets you back in touch with your inner beast as you devour the pork right off the bone. I knew you had it in you.

SERVES 8

- 2 bay leaves
- 1 teaspoon cumin seeds
- 1 teaspoon coriander seeds
- 1 teaspoon dried oregano, preferably Mexican
- 1 teaspoon black peppercorns
- 2 tablespoons rendered lard or extra-virgin olive oil
- 4½ pounds (2 kg) pork spareribs, baby back ribs, neck bones, or shoulder, cut into 2-inch pieces
- 1 medium white onion (14.7 oz/418 g), chopped
- 5 teaspoons Diamond Crystal kosher salt (0.7 oz/20 g)
- 6 medium chiles poblanos (28 oz/804 g), stemmed, seeded, and chopped
- 7 medium tomatillos (15.8 oz/449 g), husked, rinsed, and quartered
- 4 chiles jalapeños (4.6 oz/132 g), stemmed and chopped
- 6 garlic cloves, chopped
- 6 spring onions or scallions (4.6 oz/132 g), root end trimmed and thinly sliced
- ⅓ cup roughly chopped fresh cilantro leaves with tender stems (0.7 oz/20 g)

SALSA PAIRINGS

I like the nutty ones with this. Any salsa macha (pages 202 to 206), Ajonjolí (page 97), El Cacahuate (page 93).

1. In a molcajete or spice grinder, grind the bay leaves, cumin seeds, coriander seeds, oregano, and peppercorns until very finely ground. Transfer to a small bowl and set aside until ready to use.

2. In a large heavy pot, heat the lard over medium-high until very hot. Working in batches, add the ribs and cook, turning once, until browned on at least 1 side, 8 to 10 minutes. Transfer to a large bowl.

3. To the same pot, add the onion and salt and cook until the onion is browned and tender, stirring occasionally to scrape up any browned bits from the bottom of the pan, 7 to 9 minutes.

4. Add the reserved spice blend and cook until very fragrant, stirring frequently, about 1 minute. Add the poblanos, tomatillos, jalapeños, and garlic and cook, stirring occasionally, until tender and just beginning to brown, 8 to 10 minutes.

5. Add the ribs and 2 cups water and bring to a boil. Cover, reduce the heat to medium-low, and simmer until the ribs are very tender and falling off the bone, 2 to 2½ hours.

6. Let sit off the heat, covered, for about 15 minutes before serving.

7. Stir in the spring onions and cilantro. Serve with warm tortillas, arroz, and frijoles de olla.

Do ahead: The chile can be made up to 3 days ahead. Store in an airtight container in the refrigerator, or freeze for up to 3 months.

SOPA DE CHIPOTLE Y CHOCHOYOTES

SUMMER VEGETABLE SOUP WITH MASA DUMPLINGS
Summer vegetables, chipotle, and corn masa dumplings

This summery vegetable soup (and probably all summer vegetable soups in the world) is a perfect vehicle for any Salsa Macha (pages 202 to 206). You need a little kick with all that sweet veg, like corn and zucchini. The star ingredient here is really the chochoyotes, corn masa dumplings—so if you love chicken and dumplings, you'll love these. There's no chicken, but the chipotles in adobo infuse the corn dumplings with their intense, smoky flavor. But feel free to stir in 2 cups of shredded cooked chicken just before serving.

SERVES 4

- 1 cup masa harina (4 oz/112 g), any color
- 4 tablespoons rendered lard or extra-virgin olive oil, divided
- Diamond Crystal kosher salt
- ½ medium white onion (7 oz/198 g), chopped
- 1 large chile poblano (6 oz/170 g), stemmed, seeded, and chopped
- 1 medium zucchini, quartered lengthwise and thickly sliced
- 2 medium carrots, roughly chopped
- ½ pound (226 g) fresh green beans (or frozen), trimmed and halved crosswise
- 2 chipotles chiles in adobo, chopped
- 3 tablespoons adobo sauce (from the can)
- 3 garlic cloves, finely chopped
- 2 ears corn, husked and cut into 2-inch rounds, or 1 cup corn kernels (from 2 ears or frozen)

FOR SERVING

- Any Salsa Macha (pages 202 to 206)
- Chopped fresh cilantro
- Chopped onion
- Lime wedges, for squeezing

1. In a medium bowl, stir together the masa harina, 1 tablespoon of the lard, ½ teaspoon salt (0.07 oz/2 g), and ¾ cup warm water until combined and a sticky dough forms. Cover with a clean kitchen towel and let sit at room temperature for 20 minutes to allow the masa to hydrate.

2. In a large pot or Dutch oven, heat the remaining 3 tablespoons lard over medium-high. Add the onion, poblano, zucchini, carrots, green beans, chipotle, adobo sauce, garlic, and 1½ teaspoons salt (0.2 oz/6 g) and cook, stirring occasionally, until the vegetables are almost tender and just beginning to brown, 8 to 10 minutes.

3. Add the corn and cook, stirring occasionally, until the kernels are bright yellow and any liquid in the pot has evaporated, about 5 minutes.

4. Add 6 cups water and bring to a boil over high heat. Reduce the heat to maintain a low boil and cook until the vegetables are tender, about 10 minutes.

5. Meanwhile, to form the chochoyotes, scoop rounded tablespoons of the masa, roll into balls, and place on a platter or small sheet tray; you should have about 16. Cup your hand and place a ball in the center. Use your thumb to gently press down in the center of the ball to make an indentation, like a thumbprint cookie but with a rounded backside. Repeat with the remaining balls.

6. Gently add the dumplings to the pot and cook until they float to the top and are cooked through, 5 to 10 minutes. Taste and season with more salt if desired.

7. Divide the soup among bowls and serve warm with a dollop of salsa macha, a sprinkle of cilantro and onion, and a squeeze of lime.

Do ahead: The sopa can be made up to 3 days ahead. Store in an airtight container in the refrigerator.

POZOLE VERDE CON POLLO

GREEN CHICKEN AND HOMINY STEW
Hominy, tomatillo, and rotisserie chicken

Here's a quick, 45-minute pozole for your fall and winter repertoire, though let's be real, I eat it year-round, even on the hottest of days. The hominy's mild, chewy, corniness is so comforting in the tart-savory tomatillo/chile poblano stew. I save time by using rotisserie or roast chicken leftovers, and by topping it with a spoonful of the very special, sweet-savory caramelized onion salsa from page 214. Now, that salsa takes time, but in this scenario, I've made it already and am pulling it from the fridge or freezer. It's honestly a damn good pozole on its own or with any other of your favorite salsas.

SERVES 6 TO 8

- 2 tablespoons rendered lard or extra-virgin olive oil
- 2 large chiles poblanos (13 oz/367 g), stemmed, seeded, chopped
- 1 large bunch scallions (6.6 oz/187 g), root ends trimmed and roughly chopped, green and white parts kept separate
- 4 garlic cloves, peeled and smashed (but still holding their shape)
- 2 tablespoons Diamond Crystal kosher salt (0.84 oz/24 g), plus more to taste
- 1 teaspoon cumin seeds
- 1 teaspoon coriander seeds
- 7 medium tomatillos (15.8 oz/449 g), husked, rinsed, and roughly chopped
- 6 cups low-sodium chicken stock, divided
- 2 (15-ounce) cans white hominy, drained and rinsed
- 1 small bunch cilantro (1.7 oz/48 g), roughly chopped
- 2 cups shredded cooked chicken (from a roast chicken or rotisserie chicken)

FOR SERVING

- Salsa de Cebolla y Serrano Caramelizado (page 214)
- Avocado
- Cotija
- Lime wedges, for squeezing

1. In a large heavy pot, heat the lard over medium-high. Add the poblanos, scallion whites, garlic, salt, cumin seeds, and coriander seeds and cook, stirring occasionally, until just tender, about 5 minutes.

2. Add the tomatillos and continue to cook, stirring occasionally, until tender and just beginning to brown, about 6 minutes. Remove from the heat, add 1 cup of the stock, and scrape any browned bits from the bottom of the pot.

3. Carefully transfer all the vegetables and liquid to a blender and purée until completely smooth. Return the tomatillo purée to the pot. (Hold onto the blender jar, and no need to rinse.)

4. Add the remaining 5 cups stock and hominy to the pot and bring to a boil. Cover, reduce the heat to medium-low, and simmer until the broth is an olive green and the stew is very fragrant, about 30 minutes.

5. Meanwhile, in the reserved blender jar, combine the cilantro, scallion greens, and 2 cups water and blend until completely smooth.

6. Add the cilantro purée and chicken to the pozole, remove from heat, and stir to combine. Let sit until the chicken is heated through.

7. Serve the pozole with caramelized onion salsa, avocado, Cotija, and a squeeze of lime.

Do ahead: The pozole can be made up to 3 days ahead. Store in an airtight container in the refrigerator, or freeze for up to 3 months.

SOPA DE POLLO Y SALSA

Chicken stewed in salsa

I was inspired by a classic tortilla soup for this recipe, but I used a shortcut: prepared salsa. After browning onion and garlic, 2 cups of salsa help build the base of the soup (because if you think about it, they're like a packet of instant ramen seasoning, concentrated with flavor that plays well with others). I'd recommend using a salsa with tomatillos or tomatoes, or a chopped pico that can add some texture to the soup—this is not a moment for an intense fermented hot sauce, guacamole (eww), or an oily salsa macha. Follow the recipe below using really any of the table or cooked salsas, or even a combination.

SERVES 4

- 2 tablespoons extra-virgin olive oil
- 4 large bone-in, skin-on chicken thighs (1.3 lb/586 g)
- ½ medium white onion (6.1 oz/175 g), chopped
- 2 garlic cloves, finely grated
- 1 tablespoon Diamond Crystal kosher salt (0.42 oz/12 g), plus more to taste
- 2 cups salsa (see Salsa Pairings, below)
- 1 teaspoon dried Mexican oregano
- 5 cups low-sodium chicken broth

FOR SERVING

- Totopos (page 112), Tostadas (page 113), or tortilla chips
- Crema
- Crumbled queso fresco
- Chopped onion
- Chopped fresh cilantro
- Lime wedges, for squeezing

SALSA PAIRINGS

Feel free to mix and match salsas from around the book (or your personal stash); you don't need 2 cups of the same one! For this dish, I particularly like, Ensalada Picante (page 70), La Ciruela Agridulce (page 48), and La Haba Fresca (page 47).

1. In a large heavy pot, heat the oil over medium-high. Add the chicken, skin-side down, and cook until browned on both sides, 8 to 10 minutes. Transfer to a plate.

2. To the same pot, add the onion, garlic, and salt and cook, stirring occasionally, until the onion is tender and beginning to brown, 5 to 7 minutes.

3. Add the salsa and oregano and cook, stirring occasionally, until the salsa thickens slightly and darkens in color, about 5 minutes.

4. Return the chicken and any accumulated juices to the pot. Add the broth and bring to a boil. Reduce the heat to medium-low and simmer until the chicken is cooked through and the flavors have come together, about 30 minutes.

5. Ladle the soup into bowls and top with totopos or tostadas, a drizzle of crema, a sprinkle of queso fresco, chopped onion and cilantro, and a squeeze of lime.

Do ahead: The soup can be made up to 3 days ahead. Store in an airtight container in the refrigerator, or freeze for up to 3 months.

SONORAN-STYLE HOT DOGS

Hot dog, bacon, and chorizo

You've probably seen these over-the-top hot dogs before, and if you're lucky, eaten one, too. If not, imagine a hot dog wrapped in bacon and topped with everything on this planet Earth. My version is pared back, if you can believe it (this is hard for me). It stars a chorizo and bean mixture that I like to drizzle my unholy Alfredo rojo sauce over, because that spicy red crema is the definition of excess. Make these for a party and your guests will be talking about it for years after, wondering if you'll ever do it again . . .

SERVES 8

- 4 tablespoons rendered lard or extra-virgin olive oil, divided
- 4 ounces (113 g) Mexican fresh chorizo, casings removed
- ½ medium white onion (6.1 oz/175 g), chopped
- 2 garlic cloves, finely grated
- 1 (15-ounce) can black beans, undrained

    Diamond Crystal kosher salt (optional)
- 8 beef hot dogs (preferably jumbo)
- 8 thin slices bacon (4.2 oz/119 g)

FOR SERVING

- 8 soft bolillos, tops split open, or hot dog buns, warmed
- Alfredo Rojo (page 210)
- Aguacate Ahumado (page 77)
- 4 ounces (113 g) queso fresco, crumbled
- Chopped fresh cilantro
- Kettle-cooked potato chips

1. In a large skillet, heat 1 tablespoon of the lard over medium-high. Add the chorizo, breaking up any large chunks with a spoon, and cook until browned and cooked through, about 5 minutes. Transfer to a medium bowl.

2. In the same skillet, heat 1 tablespoon of the lard over medium-high. Add the onion and garlic and cook, stirring occasionally, until the onion is just beginning to brown, about 5 minutes.

3. Return the chorizo to the pan and add the beans and their liquid. Cook, stirring occasionally, until most of the liquid has evaporated, about 8 minutes. Taste and season with salt if desired. Transfer to a medium bowl. Wipe the skillet clean.

4. Wrap each hot dog with a bacon slice so that the entire hot dog is covered. In the same skillet, heat the remaining 2 tablespoons lard over medium-high. Add the hot dogs and cook, turning occasionally, until browned and crispy on all sides, 6 to 8 minutes. Transfer to a plate.

5. To serve: Nestle each hot dog in a warm bolillo. Top with the chorizo/bean mixture, a drizzle of alfredo rojo, a dollop of aguacate ahumado, the queso fresco, and cilantro. Serve with kettle chips on the side or crumbled on top.

CAMARONES AL COCO

COCONUT SHRIMP
Coconut fried shrimp and pineapple salsa

I told you La Piña (page 44) was born to be served with coconut shrimp, so I couldn't leave you stranded without a recipe. I'm spoiled with fresh shrimp in Mazatlán, so I've been able to perfect my coconut shrimp technique, and I've learned that sweetened coconut flakes are the secret. You need that hint of sugar to help the crispy coating brown, and the sweet coconut complements the sweet shrimp nicely. The salsa, of course, shows up to offer a refreshing, juicy, and hot contrast, like warming in the sun after a dip in the ocean. Some things just go together.

SERVES 4

- 1 pound (453 g) extra-large shrimp, peeled and deveined
- 1 teaspoon Diamond Crystal kosher salt (0.14 oz/4 g), plus more to taste
- 1 teaspoon freshly ground black pepper, plus more to taste
- ½ teaspoon freshly ground allspice, pumpkin pie spice, or cinnamon
- 1 cup all-purpose flour (4.4 oz/125 g)
- 2 large eggs
- 3 cups shredded dried coconut, preferably sweetened, divided

  Virgin coconut oil or vegetable oil (about 4 cups), for shallow-frying

  La Piña (page 44) or another fruity salsa (see Salsa Pairings, below); for serving

Optional equipment:
A deep-fry thermometer

FOR SERVING

- Lime wedges, for squeezing

SALSA PAIRINGS

Rick's tip: Smash the chopped salsas so they stick to the shrimp. Besitos de Kiwi (page 65), Chiles Y Nuez de la India (page 109), El Melón Mágico (page 74) Mermelada de Mole Guajillo (page 121).

1. In a medium bowl, toss the shrimp with the salt, pepper, and allspice until completely coated. Cover with plastic and refrigerate until ready to use—but for no longer than 3 hours.

2. Set up a dredging station in three shallow bowls or pie plates: Add the flour to one. Place the eggs in a bowl and beat with 1 tablespoon water to combine. Place 1½ cups of the dried coconut in a third bowl. Season the flour and eggs with salt and pepper.

3. Pour 1 inch of coconut oil into a heavy medium pot and fit with a deep-fry thermometer, if using. Heat over high until the thermometer registers 325°F.

4. Working in small batches, dredge the shrimp in the flour, turning to coat and packing into crevices. Shake to remove the excess and transfer to a sheet pan. Dip the shrimp into the egg mixture, tap against the side of the bowl to allow excess to drip off, then pack coconut firmly onto the shrimp to completely cover. Gently shake off excess and return to the sheet pan. After you have breaded about half of the shrimp, you will have used most of the coconut and what is left will be slightly wet from the egg. Discard and continue working with the remaining 1½ cups dried coconut.

5. Line a sheet pan with paper towels and set near the stove. Working in batches, fry the shrimp until golden brown, turning once, about 1 minute per side. Adjust the heat level during frying to maintain a consistent temperature. Transfer to the paper towels to drain.

6. Serve the warm shrimp on a platter with salsa and a squeeze of lime.

A BITTERSWEET GOODBYE 28

✳ I hope you enjoyed this book as much as I have making it. Writing this book has made me a better, more creative cook. I progressively felt freer with each chapter I cooked. I learned so much and wanted to pass everything on to you. My biggest hope is that you try these recipes and they inspire you to change them up and make them your own. That you start using salsa like a jar of mayo or a bottle of ketchup—put it on everything! That you see jarred salsa on the supermarket shelf and think, "pshhh I can do that (better)." That you start using your frozen salsa stash to make weeknight dinners tastier, faster, easier, and spicier than the good lord should allow. But most important, have fun and make someone smile with your food. And now, a little something sweet for the road.
Love,
Rick

BESITOS DE SALSA MACHA

SALSA MACHA KISSES

Salsa macha, piloncillo, and chocolate chunk cookies

MAKES ABOUT 20 COOKIES

- 6 ounces (170 g) grated piloncillo or dark brown sugar
- 1 stick (4 oz/113 g) unsalted butter, melted
- ⅓ cup (100 g) Salsa Macha de Vainilla y Ghee (page 206), melted, plus more for topping cookies
- ⅓ cup (67 g) granulated sugar
- ½ teaspoon Diamond Crystal kosher salt (0.07 oz/2 g)
- 1 large egg
- 2 teaspoons pure vanilla extract or vanilla paste
- 2 cups (250 g) all-purpose flour
- ½ teaspoon baking soda
- 1 heaping cup (170 g) bittersweet chocolate discs, chips, or chunks (72% cacao or higher)
- Flaky sea salt or more kosher salt

Do ahead: The cookie dough can be made up to 5 days ahead; store in an airtight container and refrigerate. Or portion into balls and freeze for up to 3 months.

1. In a large bowl, whisk together the piloncillo, melted butter, salsa macha, granulated sugar, and salt until completely combined. Vigorously whisk in the egg and vanilla until the mixture lightens in color and becomes almost ribbony, but with undissolved pieces of piloncillo and nuts, about 1 minute. This step is very important and will give your cookie a shiny, brownie-like top that will crisp as it bakes.

2. Add the flour and baking soda and, using a wooden spoon or rubber spatula, mix until the dough comes together and no floury bits remain, about 30 seconds. Stir in the chocolate until evenly distributed. The dough will be soft and may be warmer than room temperature. Refrigerate for at least 30 minutes (or up to 5 days; see Do Ahead, below) to enhance the flavor and to allow the dough to firm up.

3. Meanwhile, if baking right away, arrange a rack in the center of the oven and preheat to 350°F. Line a baking sheet with parchment paper.

4. Using a 1-ounce cookie scoop, portion out balls of dough (about 2 tablespoons each) and place on the lined baking sheet, spaced about 2 inches apart. (You can also form dough into balls the size of Ping-Pong balls with your hands.) Do not flatten; the cookies will spread as they bake. Top each ball with a pinch of salsa macha (about ¼ teaspoon) and sprinkle with sea salt or kosher salt.

5. Bake the cookies until the edges are brown and firm but the centers are still soft, 14 to 16 minutes.

6. Let the cookies cool on the baking sheet for 10 minutes, then transfer to a wire rack to cool completely.

7. Repeat with the remaining dough and a cooled baking sheet lined with parchment paper.

ACKNOWLEDGMENTS

Writing a book takes an army of talented people committed to turning your vision into a physical work of art that is both entertaining and useful. This book would not exist without the love, dedication, passion, creativity, and tireless effort of the *Salsa Daddy* team. I love you all more than these words can convey.

Alex Beggs has been a salsa fan of mine since back in the *Bon Appétit* days. She's an amazing editor and a good friend. So naturally when I decided I wanted to write a book about salsas, she was the first person I called. She helped me organize my thoughts and made my salsa scribbles make sense, and more than that, she made my professorial ramblings interesting, light, and funny. I love you, Alex Beggs.

Chris Cristiano was the second person I called. I had been asking him if he wanted to design my next book since he finished designing *Mi Cocina*. Thankfully, he said yes. Because of Chris's design, *Salsa Daddy* feels more like an extension of my soul. I did not think it was possible to love a book this much, but I do. Thank you, Chris, for completely blowing my mind, once again.

Alex Lau and I started at *Bon Appétit* at the same time. We were baby junior staffers who had to prove ourselves, me writing web recipes and Alex shooting them in a closet. The great thing about no one caring about what you do is that you can cook and shoot whatever you want. We had so much fun together, inventing projects for ourselves and pushing ourselves creatively.

I hadn't worked with him since then and was so excited to reconnect and recreate that unbridled creativity we had back then.

Caroline Hwang's food styling is nothing short of sorcery. She styled the food for *Mi Cocina* and there is no one I trust more than her with making my food jump off the page. She also is boundless in her patience and has a big, generous heart.

Jessica Darakjian assisted Caroline for both *Mi Cocina* and *Salsa Daddy* and knew exactly where to source the most beautiful and freshest ingredients in Mazatlán and kept us all well-fed for two weeks. But more than that, she's funny, quick to laugh, resourceful, an expert problem solver, and deeply kind.

Sophia Eleni Pappas, what a joy to see you work. Your prop styling is such art and watching you compose each shot, balancing the colors and surrounding the food with life and vibrancy, was inspiring and taught me a lot about my own styling.

Sam Campoli, our very own set creator, I am still OBSESSED with all of the gorgeous colored and textured surfaces you made. You added so much energy and love to this book, thank you!

And to everyone at Clarkson Potter, thank you so much for making this all possible. Francis Lam, thank you for your guidance and support from the proposal to publication. Marysarah Quinn, thank you so much for making the production process so seamless and dare I say, fun! Darian Keels and Susan Roxborough, thank you for keeping me on track and on schedule. And thank you to the amazing marketing and publicity team, Allison Renzulli, Monica Stanton, David Hawk, and Felix Cruz, for getting this book out with a bang!

Katherine Cowles, you have been my literary rock for two books and many more to come! I love you and can't wait to start book three!

Emileano (Emi) Brambila, I could not have done this without you. Thank you for keeping me sane while I was developing the recipes and you were managing the construction of the second floor. And thank you for eating gallons of salsa with me—watching you enjoy them gave me the energy to finish the book in record time!

INDEX

INDEX

Published in the United States by Clarkson Potter/Publishers,
an imprint of the Crown Publishing Group, a division of Penguin
Random House LLC, New York.
ClarksonPotter.com

Library of Congress Cataloging-in-Publication Data
Names: Martínez, Rick (Chef), author. | Lau, Alex, photographer.
Title: Salsa daddy / Rick Martinez; photographs by Alex Lau.
Description: New York: Clarkson Potter, [2025] | Includes index.
Identifiers: LCCN 2024024163 (print) | LCCN 2024024164
    (ebook) | ISBN 9780593798935 (hardcover) | ISBN
    9780593798942 (ebook)
Subjects: LCSH: Salsas (Cooking) | Dips (Appetizers) | Sauces. |
    LCGFT: Cookbooks.
Classification: LCC TX819.S29 M37 2025 (print) | LCC TX819.S29
    (ebook) | DDC 641.81/4—dc23/eng/20240910
LC record available at https://lccn.loc.gov/2024024163
LC ebook record available at https://lccn.loc.gov/2024024164

ISBN 978-0-593-79893-5
Signed edition ISBN 979-8-217-03435-2
Ebook ISBN 978-0-593-79894-2

Printed in China

Editor: Francis Lam
Editorial assistant: Darian Keels
Creative director and designer: Chris Cristiano
Art director: Marysarah Quinn
Production editor: Abby Oladipo
Production manager: Kim Tyner
Compositors: Merri Ann Morrell and Hannah Hunt
Food stylist: Caroline K. Hwang
Food stylist assistant: Jessica Darakjian
Prop stylist: Sophia Eleni Pappas
Prop stylist assistant: Samuel Campoli
Photographer: Alex Lau
Photo shoot production manager: Emileano Brambila
PR Team: Mona Creative
Copyeditor: Kate Slate
Proofreaders: Penny Haynes and Erica Rose
Indexer: Elizabeth Parson
Publicist: Felix Cruz
Marketers: David Hawk and Monica Stanton

10 9 8 7 6 5 4 3 2 1

First Edition

Rick Martínez is a celebrated Mexican American, *New York Times* bestselling cookbook author, recipe developer, and food personality. His debut book, *Mi Cocina: Recipes and Rapture from My Kitchen in Mexico,* is a James Beard Award—winner, IACP Cookbook of the Year, IACP Best International Cookbook, and *New York Times* bestseller, and serves as a transporting tribute to his family's homeland of Mexico and a personal exploration of Rick's self-identity as a third-generation Mexican American.